# I'M
# ABSOLUTELY
# FINE!

**Annabel Rivkin** and **Emilie McMeekan** founded The Midult in 2016. They are journalists, worriers and incredibly good friends. Annabel has written for everybody from *The Times* to *Vogue*, while Emilie has been Features Editor of the *Evening Standard* and Deputy Editor of *Tatler*. Together they write a Midult column in the *Saturday Telegraph Magazine* and Annabel has a column in the *Evening Standard*'s *ES Magazine*. Emilie is sunshine, Annabel is brimstone and together they wrote this book, lying on the floor a lot and stroking their beards.

# I'M ABSOLUTELY FINE!

## A MANUAL FOR IMPERFECT WOMEN

### ANNABEL RIVKIN & EMILIE McMEEKAN
#### *of* THE MIDULT

CASSELL
ILLUSTRATED

**Huge and loving thanks to**
**Gavanndra Hodge, no one shall**
**wield Excalibur but you**

An Hachette UK Company
www.hachette.co.uk

First published in Great Britain in 2018 by Cassell,
an imprint of Octopus Publishing Group Ltd
Carmelite House
50 Victoria Embankment
London EC4Y 0DZ
www.octopusbooks.co.uk

First published in paperback in 2019

ISBN 978-1-78840-172-2

A CIP catalogue record for this book
the British Library.

Printed and bound in the UK

10 9 8 7 6 5 4 3 2 1

# Contents

## Introduction

# DON'T GO MAD, GO MIDULT

WHERE ARE THE GROWN-UPS? Where are the ones who know what the hell is going on? The adultier adults? The ones who know who they are and why they are here? The thing is, if you looked at us, writing this book, you might think that we were the grown-ups. We aren't crying or quivering, or shouting, although we are obviously fucking swearing. You would never know how mad we feel most of the time. Because, most of the time, we say that we're absolutely fine.

When do we become grown-ups? When does the worry of youth subside, to be replaced by unassailable emotional equilibrium and control? There is an assumption that a numbing sets in. Even though teenagers may be repulsed, amused or disturbed by the prospect of grown-ups having feelings – lust, rage, fear, sorrow – they will find out that those tidal waves of emotion alter but do not subside. In our twenties we foresaw a dumbing down of emotion. A settling. Well, that didn't happen. *throws phone out of window* *tries to have sex with plumber* *donates £5 to Great Ormond Street* *makes self laugh* *makes self cry* We can seem so undulatingly in control, so societally functional when, in fact, we are fire-fighting feelings. Trying to look fine, be fine, feel fine. Faking it and not quite making it.

So.

What would happen, we wondered, if we actively acknowledged this endless internal combustibility; if we rifled around in our emotional knicker drawer and faced the things that we hope others will never see. The thing is, we have put on our Big Girl Pants to write this book. These Big Girl Pants give us the armour to – as Simone de Beauvoir put it – coincide with ourselves. To become who we truly are. For a moment. To taste the delicious contentment. Before it all whirligigs again and again.

Such perspective doesn't tend to strike early in life. It happens when experience, potential and an ability to say 'fuck it' come together to form a kind of knowingness. We could say 'wisdom' but then we'd have to kill ourselves. Between us, we have had alcoholism, eating disorders, PTSD, panic attacks, solo motherhood, bitter money worries, nuclear break-ups, insomnia, dead dads, nervous breakdowns, drug addictions and decades of therapy. As well as joy and conversation, proficiency and erudition, point of view and empathy.

So let's get down to business: women aged 35–55 are the healthiest, wealthiest, most emotionally intelligent and digitally literate generation of women in history. And yet we are a forgotten tribe. Who is talking to us? That group of women who grew up with grunge and rave and internet? We – Annabel and Emilie – felt as though everything directed at us was based on false assumption or lazy and out-dated marketing hypotheses. 'Busy working Mum' for example. Who's she? Does she shower in Bisto and douche with Dolmio? Why was everything that came at us – in print, online – so absolutely disconnected from how we felt?

And so we launched The Midult. As a counterproposal to all the pelvic-floor squeezing, recipes and Aga-centric oppressive worthiness all around us. As a challenge. As a connector. We launched The Midult to rebrand middle-age. Middle age had become a dress that didn't fit. If not an insult, then certainly not a compliment. Middle-age officially starts at 35 (although everyone pretends it starts at 55, just as everyone pretends menopause will only happen to other people) and it is not exactly an aspirational concept, is it? Us and our lot were roundly rejecting it as a label, which, in itself, became an act of self-loathing. We genuinely started to believe that sheer willpower could hold it at bay. It needed looking in the eye. Where was the edge? Where was the laughter? Why should we be extinguished? Why couldn't we aspire to grow into ourselves?

The Midult was born as a website and a newsletter; as a generation-defining tribe where – for once – it doesn't matter if there are kids or not. The Midult is an initiative born out of friendship. Before we knew what we wanted to do, we knew we wanted to do it together. We absolutely love each other and it is a relationship born and blossomed in the workplace. So The Midult has its roots in the redemptive power of female friendship. If you want to be schlocky. But enough of that.

Are we just working through our own midlife crises? Perhaps. But we are less interested in massive calamities than we are in crossroads. All the tiny ones that happen in every minute of every day. All the choices, all the triggers, all the dreads and mini-obsessions. All the texture and all the silly, odd, eccentric, private things that we think and do. After all, we are all savages on the inside. We may act out a little less than we did, but we are just as reactive. Like toddlers. With mortgages. And pigmentation. Does this sound familiar?

*Someone has hurt my feelings and I am holding a massive grudge. I only refer to them by their full name and I do not wish them well.*

*I need my hand held. Metaphorically. I do not know that I need my hand held but then someone – metaphorically – DARES to hold my hand and I feel a bit less at sea.*

*I can't do anything. I just can't, I just can't, I just can't. I'm hungry and I can't concentrate, I don't know what I want to eat and I might not eat just to make it worse. Today, I am basically three. I have no emotional regulation, no ability to self-soothe, I am low-level vengeful and not to be trusted. I am not able to properly look after myself and I might cry, hit or slightly wet myself at any point. I am hot. I am cold. I like you. I hate you. I am JEALOUS. Everyone has better toys.*

*My inner maniac has taken hold of the wheel and put her tiny foot down and God knows what is going to happen next. I am a liability but it really isn't hormonal. For once. Or tiredness. For twice. It just is what it is. Pure, spiky vulnerability. Maybe we should add this to our support-arsenal? What about a simple, 'So, are you basically three today?' YES YES YES. Thank God someone understands.*

'Is it just me?' We gnaw on that don't we? It is the question that feeds the ravenous brainworm of loneliness. 'Is it just me?' Look around. Look at the egg freezing, the brain-freezing, the terror, the Tinder, the rage, the resolution, the 'hear me roar'. The career-crises, the desperate desire for reset, the money panic, the laughter. The divorce, the shame, the chin hairs, the regret, the power, the hyper-connectedness, the incredible anxiety, the sheer fucking potential. Welcome to Midulthood, a place where we recognise that we are more alike than we are unalike. And that we are all doing our best. *Doing* our best rather than getting hung up on *being* our best. We may or may not be activists but at least let us acknowledge that we can be active.

Midulthood is a mood. Maybe it's a movement. But rest assured, it is not just you. It is never just you. It isn't just you who wonders what will happen next and if you'll be up to it. Or if anything will happen next…if anything will ever change. Longing for change, fearing change. And it isn't just you triggered from sunny into sad by…Oh fuck, it happened so quickly you don't even know why you were (relatively) relaxed 12 seconds ago and you are miserably murderous now. And threatened. And superior. Yet utterly, utterly less than. And still you say you're fine.

It is never just you. People are unique but feelings are not unique. They can batter us all at once like a torrential emotional storm – the good, the bad and the corrosive. And the funny. The appallingly funny. Of course it's not just you. That's why The Midult is here. If we're not in it together, we're not in it at all.

# How Should You Use This Book?

HOWEVER YOU WANT. You've had enough people telling you what to do in your life. However is useful or amusing. We have written who we are and what we know. Everything in this book has sprung out of conversation, so presumably some bits will resonate with you and others won't – but someone somewhere thinks it or feels it. There are bits of therapeutic thinking, some very mad jokes, a lot of chat and some heartache. The colours of our rainbow.

We very much hope you like it because you have inspired it. Take what you like and leave the rest. This is not a self-help book. And yet, we hope it helps.

## Welcome to Midulthood

# 20 THINGS YOU KNOW IF YOU'RE A MIDULT

1.  Nothing good happens at three in the morning.
2.  You should never buy the smallest size you can fit into.
3.  Everyone needs therapy.
4.  Grey hair is beautiful, grey roots make you look deranged.
5.  Time flies.
6.  You are probably a little bit of an alcoholic. Unless you are actually an alcoholic, in which case you may have given up drinking.
7.  You are always hungry.
8.  If you check out of technology, you are checking out of life. Don't do it.
9.  If someone has no old friends, there is a problem.
10. Infidelity doesn't necessarily mean it's over. Contempt does.
11. Things get stuck in your teeth.
12. Something always hurts.
13. And then you think it's cancer.
14. You know more and less at the same time. You think they might cancel each other out. So where does that leave us?
15. Good sleep is better than good sex.
16. Moths make you panic. Even talking about them makes you panic. MOTHS. PANIC.
17. You have 25 different kinds of herbal tea. You don't much like any of them. You'd rather have a Diet Coke. But you probably won't.
18. Swearing fucking helps.
19. This is the rush hour of life: we have spots, wrinkles and possibly braces.
20. If you need to cancel, you need to cancel.

## Chapter 1

# WHERE THE WILD THOUGHTS ARE

WARNING. IN THIS CHAPTER, we are going to press the bruise a bit. Things are going to get shady, before they get sunny. So let's dive in with a question: how mad are you feeling right now? Maybe you are perfectly balanced in every way: calm, collected and commanding; healthy, wealthy and wise. Or maybe you have a funny pulse behind one of your eyelids and you're so agitated you feel as though your heart might melt and dribble moltenly down your solar plexus. Perhaps you have given up on 'being still for a moment' and become a kind of battery-operated human toy with no soul. But I bet that – on the whole – no one would ever know. I bet that you, with your aplomb, with your meetings, dinners, commutes and conversations, are part of the sanity subterfuge that we collectively collude on. Or that we used to collectively collude on. Welcome to the Age of Anxiety. It's the glue that binds us together. Anxiety; our constant companion.

I was brought up knowing that I didn't want to be neurotic. Neurosis, like the Victorians and their hysteria, was a one-size-fits-all stick with which to whack any woman who couldn't seem to get comfortable with her lot. It was a way to handle the repulsion that struggle can elicit. A way to brand that messy bundle of womany feelings that offer some respite from nice female femininity. 'She's a neurotic,' people would say with a dismissive shrug, thereby rendering that woman's feelings unreasonable, pathetic and incurable. 'Nerves' was another one. As though, for these nervy women, life was one, long self-dramatising bout of stage fright. It was sexist, of course it was. But now, I'm told, men get it too. So that's OK then.

Naturally, with my privilege and fear of being The Neurotic, I didn't really take my overactive worry engine seriously. What did I have to worry about? I was clothed and fed and employed and healthy and housed. But anxiety doesn't care. It turns thoughts into threats.

For years, throughout adolescence and on into university and through my twenties and way into my thirties, I thought I 'had' depression. It was my badly kept secret as I fiddled around with Prozac (first prescribed at 19, last prescribed at 41) and, where possible, swerved my feelings. My default setting was dread – how could I dare to hope? Wasn't hope idiotic? Didn't it just roll out the red carpet for pain?

Through narrowed eyes, I glanced back at my childhood and found that my memory was oddly blank: atmospheric rather than actual, implied rather than remembered.

I recalled a small girl swimming around in clandestine worry. An eight-year-old weighed down by apprehension and control. Not that you would have known from the theatrical, precocious disguise that I wore. No one knew. My performance was that good. Depression, I accepted, was in my genes. My father had manic depression, although he never accepted it, and I modelled myself in his dynamic image so I had it too. Oh well. Pass the meds, why don't you?

But guess what – and this is super-annoying – mis-prescribed medication doesn't work. Punchy in the office but isolated at home, turbo-charged with adrenaline but deranged from lack of sleep, hugely confident to behold yet increasingly viewing each day as a prison sentence, I dragged myself off to see an internationally renowned expert. 'Oh, you're sad,' he said, 'of course you're sad, but what we need to treat is the anxiety disorder.'

Well. Clearly the internationally renowned expert had me all wrong. No, no, no, Man Who Knows Everything About Mental Health. No, no, no, I 'have' depression. I don't 'have' anxiety. I'm not having panic attacks, I'm just living with a lively depression that follows me wherever I go, doesn't think I deserve to sleep and is robbing me of a future because what has yet to happen is appallingly terrifying. A depression that encourages me to back myself into a dark, cold corner regarding every decision – however small – that needs making, and I end up thinking about death all the time because this spiky bleakness is so painful, so painful, so painful. A depression that is slowly cutting off the blood supply to my most essential relationships. My mother keeps telling me how frightening and intimidating I am when all I feel is frightened and intimidated. My best friend is furious that I won't stay out past 10pm because I never sleep past 3am and being out of the house at night has started to make me panic. A partner says, 'I find it so hard to watch what you do to yourself,' and then, when all I can do is glare at him or cry, helpfully leaves. And I cry more and more. And I can't stop crying. And it's not cleansing weeping. It's grating, raw, bottomless grief and these tears beget tears and there is no catharsis. I am in therapy but my therapist looks at her notes and says, 'Sure, you're under pressure. But the maths doesn't work – the component parts don't add up to this overwhelming worry.' And it doesn't ebb and flow. It just, grimly, is. Doing only damage. So, guys, apparently this is Anxiety.

You'd think that, at the age I have reached, with the amount of therapy I've had and the sheer, dull variety of 'depressive' episodes I have endured (I could say survived, but that's a bit melodramatic) well, you'd think that I'd be sitting here jiggling my fat bag of healthy coping mechanisms. I should, by rights, be fully tooled-up. And yet, am I alone in feeling that, beneath my uniform of full-functionality, lurks a maniac capable of ripping someone's fucking head off if they look at me askance? In reality I would be more likely to blushingly apologise if they stepped on my toe. But the point is, you do not have to behave like a madwoman to feel like a madwoman and to suffer like a madwoman.

'Let's,' says the incredibly distinguished doctor, 'just try another way.' And so I leave with a new and uncomfortable diagnosis. I am not a depressive. I am…an anxious person. Catchy, no? Well, yes. In another sense. Anxiety is deeply infectious and we are swimming in a pandemic of the stuff. The Age of Anxiety delivers curated lies through social media, tremendous expectation, hyper-communication – counter-intuitively blended with isolation. Worry is the new smallpox. Citalopram the new penicillin.

And so, now snugly wrapped in my new label, I glance back at that dramatic, noisy little girl. Only the bullies at primary school could tell I was vulnerable. No one else knew. It was my secret shame. But shame cannot survive being spoken. And so if we all look our anxiety in the eye and turn him (yes, him, so sue me) on his bony little head then anxiety can become – if not actually fun – then at least funny. With the Big Girls, the ones who have some murk and bruising and struggle running through their veins, it is the language of our tribe. Until recently our social understanding of the word 'anxious' did not match the immensity and intensity of the feeling. The way it can life-flatten and life-threaten.

Is it just me? Is it just you? Running on empty? Out of juice? Out of ideas? Out of everything? Never. It is part of the texture of life, this low-level lunacy. So, share the crazy. Find someone who doesn't stare at you blankly when you say, 'I am clearly going to die alone.' Find someone who laughs and says, 'But you promised to nurse me through my Alzheimer's. At least you'll know you're dying alone.' That way connection lies. And through connection comes hope.

## I'm More Sensitive Than You

Me: The thing is, I'm pretty sensitive.
You: I'm pretty sensitive too.
Me: Like, REALLY sensitive.
You: I'm so sensitive.
Me: Literally everything makes me cry.
You: Just talking about crying is making me so upset.
Me: Even the idea of watching the news is just…
You: If I ever watched the news, I think I would genuinely die.
Me: And OMG, those vet programmes…
You: I'm actually tearing up.
Me: I accidentally saw one episode where they injected this snake called Margaret and I cried and cried.

You: UNBEARABLE FOR MARGARET.

Me: Why do animals have to suffer?

You: OK, you might as well be repeatedly stabbing my chest cavity open with a butter knife, that's how much pain I'm in right now.

Me: I wish I were less sensitive. I wish I felt LESS, you know?

You: I wish I loved less. I just love so much.

Me: I have so much love that I'm surprised I am able to even breathe.

You: The love I feel for others is almost barbaric in its extremeness.

Me: I mean, I hate how much I love.

You: I have so much love it has ruined my whole life.

Me: I feel so isolated by my sensitivity.

You: I literally have no friends because I'm too sensitive.

Me: Like, I mind about EVERYTHING.

You: If I minded more about things, I would be sectioned.

Me: I actually feel envious of people less sensitive than me.

You: I mean, I'm envious of you.

Me: Errr...I don't think you would be if you were inside my head.

You: I can imagine myself inside your head. Because I'm so sensitive.

Me: Right. OK – so what am I thinking of right this second?

You: You know...something sad.

Me: WRONG. I was thinking of a sunset. Which made me feel gratitude, actually.

You: (crying)

Me: Yes, I was about to cry too.

You: (still crying) Sorry, I can't...(flaps hands in front of face)

Me: (also crying) I know, I know.

You: It's just...you know?

Me: I really do.

You: Do you though?

Me: More than you'll ever know.

You: I knew you'd say that. I'm very sensitive to what people are going to say.

Me: (cries)

You: (cries)

## Slightly On The Tense Side?

Some people are not entirely relaxed and that is fine. It's just the way we're engineered. Us slightly more vigilant types have many qualities. We are always prepared. We shimmer with alertness and adrenaline. Just not relaxed. Relaxation is not the point of us. We are too tense ever to…

- Sleep on a train – what kind of psychopath can sleep on a train with lights blaring and other people and thundering train sounds and a handbag that could be snatched?
- Wear sexy underwear – without feeling that I have to a) apologise b) make a joke of it c) pretend it's some old thing I've had forever.
- Say yes to a head massage in a hairdresser – please just wash my hair and let me get the hell out of here.
- Enjoy a hammock – a triumph of hope over experience. Getting in, getting out, enough said.
- Ditto deckchairs. Will today be the day I irreparably shatter my coccyx?
- Get a pet – a cat maybe. But the cat will die. Get run over or savaged by a fox. I am already a bit sad about the cat I have never met. Poor dead cat. Poor me.
- Remain silent during a massage – I salute those who can lie down and drift off and not ask the masseuse about her life and her star sign.
- Go out wearing no knickers. The sheer vulnerability of the proposition is not for me. Not at all.
- Park in underground car parks. Tiny spaces. Squeaky, screechy, rubbery floor. Pillars everywhere. Cameras everywhere. Murderers everywhere.
- Enjoy a picnic. Where is the nearest loo? Where is the nearest table? Is there shade? How am I going to eat this? Sorry, where is the loo?
- Leave my coat in a restaurant. I might be cold. I might need to leave in a hurry. There might be a fire. And what if they lose it?
- Do anything at the airport. Just have to sit still and stare – unblinking – at the departures board. God forbid I should miss the boarding announcement by even a nanosecond. And once the gate is announced then go, go, go. No time for Boots or Pret or Sunglass Hut. Are you insane?
- Sit alone at a café on a pavement. What am I? French?

# Time To Name And Shame Our Inner Demons

You are finally just beginning to pretend to relax. Nothing to stop you getting plenty of rest tonight…oh wait, here come all your inner demons. Such a dedicated lot. There's…

## Martin The Money Demon

Martin is a bit of a jobsworth. He likes to clock in at around 3am. His current theme is the mortgage and how you are never going to pay it off and he likes to talk and talk about all that money, yes all that money you've spent and why you haven't got a pension. Martin is a dull demon. But a highly effective one.

## Alan The Alzheimer's Demon/Lee The Death Demon

Alan has been around a lot lately because you have been watching Alzheimer's porn (*Iris, The Notebook*) and frankly at this moment, given you cannot remember anything at all ever, you are more afraid of Alan than Lee. But you'd never tell Lee that. Because he can be a bit spiteful.

## Simon The You've Always Been Bad In Bed Demon

Simon needs you to know that, when you were young and had a desperate-to-please porn film playing in your head, it was all a bit mannered and embarrassing. Everyone thought so. And he is keen to stress, now you are old and experienced, you are merely old. He needs you to realise that your tricks are pathetic and that everyone says so: 'You think you have moves? You don't have moves. In fact, you don't even move.'

## Angus The Ageing Demon

'You will never look untired again,' whispers Angus. He has a Scottish accent. 'And you are starting to look like a man. And sound like a man. And you know that running away fund you have secretly stashed? Use it for a full facelift or people will start running away from you. Also…a nose strimmer? I'll just leave you with that thought…'

## Paul The Property Demon

The crash, the crash, the crash. Paul whizzes up, in his metaphorical Lexus, to remind you that, if you had balls, you would have sold six months ago to rent for two years and then pounce, vulture-like, on all the bargains. But you do not have balls. You have never had balls.

## Tarquin The Travel Demon

Tarquin has just come back from six months in Patagonia and he just can't believe

WHERE THE WILD THOUGHTS ARE

you are still stuck here, in the suburbs, lying in bed staring at the ceiling, sun-starved and depleted and frankly a bit scaly from all that time spent in opaque tights rather than following your star to Nova Scotia. Because that's where he's going next. You are trapped. He is free. That much is clear. Can't you at least get your helix pierced?

### Colin The Cancer Demon

Colin likes the small pains the best. He likes to just nudge the brain from the slightly sore throat towards the family history and back again – via the 20 a day that you smoked at university. Colin is a joy sucker, extracting the yum from every glass of wine, every slice of salami, every grain of refined sugar.

### Ian The Imposter Demon

If Ian is around it means you've got a job interview (get you), a major presentation (yikes), a meeting with investors (not going to go well), a pay review (ha ha ha). Ian is a bit of a mansplainer too. He doesn't think you understand anything. Oh God, he's right.

### Yolanda The You're-An-Embarrassment Demon

Yolanda never draws breath: 'Why did you say that? Why did you even open your mouth? You are an idiot. And you sounded mean. No one cares if you didn't MEAN to be mean because you sound mean. And jealous. Your voice doesn't help. Reedy. Thin. Pointless. Dickish. I hate your laugh. Everyone hates your laugh.'

### Ramona The Romance Demon

'Clearly, in order to make yourself in any way loveable, you need to change,' says Ramona as she sips a Molotov cocktail. It's not them. It's you. You are falling short. You are broken. There is something missing in you. You may never find love. And then you and Ramona can be together, alone, forever.

## Is Impatience Eating My Soul?

In my head I have already finished writing this and I'm on to something else that hasn't been done. WHY hasn't it been done? What is WRONG with everybody (me)? Why is everyone so fucking leisurely?

Impatience. Sitting in the back of cabs radiating fury. Hopping from foot to foot while the toast is toasting. Drumming fingers in a waiting room. Swearing at the frozen parking app. Spit it out. Get on with it. Why are you driving like a GIRL? I get sexist when I'm impatient. It blurs my faculties. It cuts my smile muscles. I cannot laugh when things are running slightly behind.

This is about control and desperately trying to keep chaos at bay. It is about genuinely feeling that if I am late for a meeting because the cab driver doesn't know his high street from his station road then all hell will break loose and my life will unravel around me like so much wire wool.

Impatience is incredibly unattractive and corrosive and unpleasant to be around. It is chilly and brutal and unsympathetic, but the next time you find yourself being sighed at and prodded and needled by someone like me, however annoying and self-indulgent and oppressive that may be, know this: being impatient is sad and unpleasant. You enjoy very little because you are panicking about what comes next. Basically, 'the journey' is fucked. Impatience doesn't come and go, it sits on your shoulder judging, clouding, winding you up into a terrible frenzy. Impatience, like jealousy, does nothing for no one. And meditation doesn't help.

## 10 Things You Only Know If You Are In Therapy

1.  Avoid all men who say, '…and I turned out alright.' They didn't.
2.  You can recover from your childhood but not escape it.
3.  Talking about your therapeutic process in public is dull for EVERYONE.
4.  It's the only place in the world where you never need to worry about being boring.
5.  'That is not OK' is a truly useful phrase.
6.  Don't try and make friends with your shrink (if you succeed, they are rubbish).
7.  Boundaries are not just things that complete wankers talk about.
8.  You are always curious about your shrink's sex life.
9.  You are not fine, and that's OK.
10. Good therapists tend to be scary. It's up to you to work out if this is helpful.

## My Brain Has Too Many Tabs Open

What was I saying? What were you saying? What was I doing? Why am I here? In this room? Holding a spoon?

What was the thing I said I'd do? What was that idea I had? About a present for my birthday? About a present for your birthday? About a book I thought I could write? About a cake I thought I might bake? About a restaurant I thought we could try?

Who was that person I said I'd call? About a will? About a plumber? About a…Oh, you get it.

And, while we are on the subject, when was the last time you tried to charge your phone by putting it in the fridge? Or maybe you put your wallet in the petrol station bin and trotted off to the tills to pay using the bag of rubbish still clutched in your hot little hand? Have you posted your keys instead of a birthday card? Have you said 'I love you' at the end of a conference call? Do you smile absently at strangers in the street because your brain has just decided to disconnect itself from your face? Then there is giving the wrong name when you introduce yourself, which is truly peculiar. But happens.

Perhaps it is because our brains are too full, that is why we forget things, misplace things, mix things up, have to stop thinking for quite extended periods of time. As life fills to bursting with joy and stress and anxiety, is this some kind of cerebral survival technique? When heads get too full perhaps consciousness takes flight for a while to preserve capacity. Or – oh God – it could well be the opposite: some sinister indication of failing faculty. But we're not going to think about that, although maybe we should take up elasticity-encouraging Sudoku to massage the grey matter into motion.

Or is it the fault of the phones, and how very distracted they have made us, and how very addicted we have become to the distraction because the people in charge employed clever, evil psychologists to empty our minds of everything useful and fill them instead with nonsense and the compulsion to touch a glassy screen and see more nonsense when instead we might be listening to a friend, looking at a view of a mountain, closing our eyes and thinking, deeply, serenely. Attention spans have dropped from 12 seconds in the year 2000 to 8 seconds today. Goldfish, by the way, have an attention span of 9 seconds.

But, the strange truth is that despite the forgetfulness, the distractedness, the confusedness, I am just about getting by. Not that organised. Not that dynamic. But above water. In fact, the forgetfulness seems to have removed a whole layer of stress. Can't remember what needs doing = don't worry about what needs doing. Apart from that nagging feeling that my life is slithering through the cracks in my Swiss cheese brain. Sorry, what was I worrying about? See? Quite relaxing…

# Things We Think About On The Loo

You'd think that the throne might be sacred. A break. Some sweet release. Particularly since we seem to spend more and more time here. But, it seems, the fun never stops. Even if we've conquered our pelvic floor (ha), the mental incontinence prevails. Leaky brains, busy, busy, busy with…

1.  I was here ten minutes ago. Is it normal for a human bladder to be the size of a lentil?
2.  Is that a grey pube? Can it be? Already? *waggles hips from side to side to try and establish whether it is a trick of the light*
3.  Did I buy a EuroMillions lottery ticket for today? If I did, why can't I remember that I did? Where did I put it? What if I win and I don't know because I don't know

where I put it or even if I have it at all? Is this early onset Alzheimer's?

4. Am I drinking too much water? Am I going to end up overdosing like Anthony Andrews that time he drank eight litres in one day because it was hot and then collapsed?

5. Is my parking running out???

6. Why don't I fancy Idris Elba? Is there something wrong with me? Should I confess? No, I can't. *thinks of all the times I nodded and mouthed 'hot' when his name came up*

7. How long before they notice I am gone? Because I have my phone.

8. Why is the person in the next-door cubicle peeing so quietly? Why am I peeing like a racehorse? Social peeing anxiety.

9. If I have a micro-sleep that turns into a full-blown sleep by accident and I have to be busted out of this cubicle because they think I've died, I'm not wearing knickers that really represent who I am today. This is so unfair and misleading.

10. Pelvic floor exercises, pelvic floor exercises, pelvic floor exercises.

## The Problem With Angry Birds

Women are not meant to be angry, they said. Makes us seem…rabid. Female fury is ugly (apparently) to men, to children, to other women, even to furry animals. This is what we have been told and taught, all our lives. There is something unnatural and unnerving about the angry woman. Madwoman. Bitch. Harridan. No one wants to fuck the activist, no one will love you if you are shouting. This is sounding quite angry already. What a turn-off.

And the problem we are left with, because we were good little learners and we yearned to be loved, is that as grown-ups we don't know how to deal with the anger when it rises up in us, as of course it has and does and will. Perfectly justified but not recommended. We don't know how to manage it and deliver it usefully. So we bottle it and contain it and add to it with each new fucking angry-making thing, so it grows and mutates. The ones who are virtuoso at bottling, who put on their pretend happy face while inside they are shaking, are liable to suffer an explosion that will leave bits of them stuck to the walls. But I am not good at bottling. Instead I find that I am a little bit angry all the time; minor irritation radiating out of every pore. Some weeks are worse than other weeks. Some weeks I am more dangerous than other weeks. A risky proposition, constantly to be triggered in a thin-skinned, hormonal, haven't slept, the loo-is-leaking-through-the-kitchen-ceiling, indigestion kind of a way. And I am ashamed, I think it is my fault, I ask people to forgive me and my horrible personality. And then I worry that they can't and they won't and friends will fall away and I will end up not just solitary, but lonely, and anxiety becomes heaped on top of anger and I am somewhere underneath it all, barely able to breathe.

I say sorry, I'm stressed; sorry, I'm hungry; sorry, I'm insecure, vulnerable, tired. I never say, 'Sorry, I'm just angry.' Anything but angry; the word is red, dangerous, unacceptable. But, I do find myself disproportionately angry about things that really shouldn't make me feel angry – burnt toast, moth hole in jumper, slow tourist walking in front of me – any kind of momentary impediment or minor setback makes me incandescent. And, by the end of the day, when I turn to look at myself in the mirror, I see a clenched jaw and find myself incapable of unclenching it. I realise that it is not new, disproportionate anger that makes me look and feel this way, it is that old, proportionate, unexpressed anger. So maybe I need to undergo a sort of self-devised free-style anger programme. To practise saying, 'I am angry.' To myself, to others, to the world. I am angry. And my anger, expressed and heard, might be the thing that will help me feel less angry.

# All The Therapists We've Had

### The Brute
Fierce, this one. No hiding behind your depressing story or the obvious rant about the daily indignities. No telling charming jokes. No getting anything past the brute. You dread every visit, cry futile tears to stop the remorseless probing and feel better than you have done in years. Probably ever.

### The Man
Oh, the novelty. A man. How grown-up. Because you are feeling so much more in control of all the Daddy stuff now and it's been a really long time since you had an inappropriate crush. Really it makes you feel a bit cool, a bit edgy, to have a male therapist. Like having a male masseur. Or a 'manny'. Then you find you want to make him laugh and wonder if he thinks about you when you are not there and realise it's a very bad idea.

### The Mother
She is so lovely to you. So kind. So thoughtful and considered and listens and so patient and understanding and not judgey or snarky or defensive. She has at least six clocks dotted around the room so you never know when she is looking at the time as you drone on about the imposter syndrome and why you are fixated by the blob on your face that no one else can see. Her cushions are so cosy. She's so NICE, your new mother. You wonder if you are actually learning anything at all...

**The Academic**

She is German, of course she is. Everything is Freudian. Or Jungian. Exhaustingly so. 'I don't know why I like spoons better than forks,' you howl. 'I can't remember my fucking dreams,' you scream. You try to sack her and she won't let you go. For two years. She also charges you when she goes on holiday, which you think is very unfair but are too afraid to bring up. Retrospectively you think she might have been the crazier one.

**The Group**

Something incredibly weird happens when you sit down in the group. You feel oddly supported. You love them all. And everything resonates so much. And you identify madly with everything. Except. Isn't she quite annoying? And why is he moaning? And I hate her shoes. Not the 'trip to the seaside' story again. You are reminded that you are a terminally terrible person. But that one's quite hot.

# Medication, Medication, Medication

'So are you on Citalopram or Cipralex and how long do the side effects last and did the pills make you fat and did you get heart palpitations and how many milligrams?'

That was a text, recently sent, from one Midult to another. Confidentially.

'Well actually they've put me on something called Vortioxetine, which is a kind of new-gen Prozac and apparently it doesn't mess with your sex drive although I'm not sure that's enough of a boon to compensate for the nausea and insomnia. Hopefully it won't make me put on a stone like the Citalopram did. I was thinking of white knuckling it for the summer and just banging the odd beta blocker when I felt really insane but I'm giving these a go for six weeks. Might as well,' came the lengthy reply.

The word 'meds', on text, autocorrects as 'mess'. Which is obviously apt, because they are what you take when you are in one. A mess. A pickle. A heap. And once you know they know you know, they know you know they know you both know you are on them, it becomes a fertile furrow to plough. 'I don't think I am managing my reactions properly, so is it right to be on an SSRI or should I be on anti-anxiety meds?' Hmmm, interesting question. It gets quite cliquey, because bonding over drugs ('I've cut down to one 20mg a week, which traditional medical wisdom would have you believe only offers a placebo effect but I swear it's a mini-lifebuoy') is more binding than bonding over bad boyfriends or bosses. Because it dissolves the self-reproach. And it's completely compelling. Pill talk – the gift that keeps on giving...

# The Rich Tapestry Of Tears

### Angry Tears

You are so monumentally cross, so annoyed, so enraged, so infuriated – it's as if you've stubbed your soul on the bottom of the bed and you are standing there with balled fists and angry water is leaking out of your eyes. They could bottle this water and give it to other women who have trouble accessing their fury. It could be administered via a low-fat, sugar-free salad dressing.

### Hungry Tears

It doesn't matter why you are this hungry – mismanaged lunchtime, hormonal explosion, silly diet – but you are encountering a small bump in the road of your day, and you can only think 'chicken, chicken, chicken'. And then you start to cry. There is a subset of this which is 'still hungry tears', as in you've eaten a pig and a cake and the fridge, why are you still hungry? *howls*

### Cleansing Tears

The best kind of crying. The one where you feel better, really better, not weirdly worse afterwards. You do it on purpose: a full-bodied, full-faced explosion. Perhaps you engineered it by watching *Steel Magnolias*. Perhaps it happened during acupuncture in front of a practitioner who made a 'this often happens' proud face. Either way, you feel lighter and brighter for it. A cry-win.

### Yoga Tears

Not a cleansing cry. Or a primal howl. More of an awful, I can't remember how to breathe and this yoga mat is smelly and why am I here? Please don't touch me with your toe.

### Teen Romance Tears

Oh, the tears we have shed. The Alice in Wonderland-ish rivers. The listening to lugubrious ballads, over and over again. This is no ordinary love. You may not remember his name but you'll never forget the pain.

### Touched Tears

Someone is telling you a sad story and all of a sudden you are overcome with empathy and connection, and it's really quite embarrassing but you are beginning to well up, and the sad story is not remotely happening to you but the interlocutor is suddenly trying to comfort you and you are doing that jaw-tightening thing to try and make it stop.

**Wardrobe Tears**
When you open your cupboard, stare at the inside for a bit and then throw a tantrum of epic proportions. You will definitely stamp your feet, you might even say 'it's not fair'. And it bloody isn't. You leave the house in the same 'jeans and a top' you always wear.

**Comic Relief Tears**
One minute you are laughing at French and Saunders, next there's a child on screen dying of malaria and there is snot streaming down your chin and you have texted £100 to Comic Relief and then you guiltily turn it off and watch reruns of *Grand Designs* instead because you can't bear it even though you should but you can't.

**Defeated Tears**
When you feel as bleak and exhausted as a silent French movie actress walking the rainy streets of Paris with just a beret and a broken heart for company. You are empty. You are nothing. *Rien.*

**Unprofessional Tears**
When someone in the office reworks something you put together, or 'borrows' an idea, or you are not invited to a higher-ups meeting, and you know you are bigger than this, but you are still sitting in the disabled loo wiping snot from your nose and writing your resignation letter and cursing yourself for being so feeble and cursing them for being such fuckers. These tears sting.

**Happy Tears**
The thing about happy tears is that you keep having to say 'happy tears, happy tears' while you flap your hands in front of your face and hear your voice getting higher and higher: 'No, honestly, these are happy tears.' And everyone thinks you are insane.

## Shrink Etiquette

1.  Don't ask them about their sex life. In fact, don't ask them about their life at all. If they answer it will be because they have decided to collude with you on pretending to have a normal conversation. It will be awkward. This is the only situation where you should only talk about yourself.
2.  You can't really touch them. If you want to, you'd better ask first. (Also good advice for life.) They are fully tooled-up when it comes to boundaries. But if things get really bad they might give you a pat on the shoulder.
3.  If you have friends who share your therapist – which is both an act of kindness and

insanity – they will take a very dim view if you say things like, 'How's Meg doing?' They don't like it. They pride themselves on keeping things separate. They may even say something chilling like, 'What's your point?'

4.  In the end, you have to talk about your mother. You can't just lie there and cry.

5.  You can ask for a break. We don't mean like a fag break in the middle of the session (although some won't mind if they think it might calm you the fuck down and that is what is needed in order for them to get you out the door in one piece in 21 minutes' time) but rather a shrink sabbatical.

6.  Don't bring food. Drinks are fine. Munching and spraying crumbs is not. Get organised – eat an energy bar as you walk up the stairs.

7.  No social media. You can't live tweet your therapy session or Instagram the couch. That just makes you a dick.

8.  They don't like it when you are late. They say it's because you are cheating yourself out of time. Or that there must be a deep-rooted reason why you felt the need to be late. Lateness offends them and they will take it to their shrink. Every shrink has a shrink. It's the law.

9.  Never say, 'I think I am better. In fact, I think I might be done.' They'll have you in tears within five minutes. Just because they can.

10. If it's not working, it might be them not you. Find another one. (Good advice for life too.)

# I'm More Hormonal Than You

Me:  Is it me or is it fucking boiling in here?

You: I mean, it's literally a furnace in the burning mouth of Hell.

Me:  Do I have steam coming off the top of my head?

You: I can't see, I'm too depressed.

Me:  Well, try depressed and ANGRY FOR NO REASON.

You: Please don't shout, it might make me cry.

Me:  You're talking like I can control any of this. I can't control any of this.

You: It's hard to concentrate on what people are saying when you haven't slept, like, ever.

Me:  I know you're staring at my terrible skin.

You: I can't even see your skin, I'm too upset.

Me:  SHUT UP. Sorry, I have no idea where that came from.

You: Do my boobs look massive and painful to you?

Me:  Do I look 20 stone heavier to you?

You: (crying)

Me: Why are you crying?

You: How should I know?

Me: (also crying)

You: And now I've made you cry. I'm a terrible person who should be living a solitary life in a cave away from others.

Me: OMG this headache.

You: I gave you a headache. I am evil and must be destroyed.

Me: Wow, are you still talking? STOP TALKING DON'T MAKE ME KILL YOU. Sorry, that just came out.

You: If I'm not eating chocolate of some description within the next four seconds, I am going to get violent.

Me: Sugar is my only food group at the moment.

You: Give me chocolate or I will SMASH THIS PLACE UP…Sorry.

Me: My basal temperature is so high I can melt a bar of chocolate just by walking into the same room as it.

You: (crying) I just want a 12-hour nap. Is that too much to ask?

Me: You know what, I'm even hairier than I was when we started this conversation.

You: And I have yellow eyes and fangs and it's not even full moon.

Me: I'm sweatier than Blanche DuBois and twice as mad.

You: (crying) I just want to watch *Beaches*.

Me: (also crying) I've never seen *Beaches*.

You: (crying) Me neither.

## When You Think Everything Is Cancer

Headache? Cancer. Sore throat? Cancer. Strange nodule on hip which might just be impressive cellulite? Cancer. Strange need to lie down because of extreme tiredness? Cancer. Not a hangover. Not too much work/sugar/life. Do not pass go, just go straight to cancer.

I am doing this a lot these days. Diagnosing myself with cancer at the very smallest twinge. It's a terrible thing, a pointless thing to do. Ignorant, really.

When I went travelling we used to laugh about the fact that all the symptoms of tropical diseases were the same as the common cold. Now, 20 years on, this is again applicable to my daily life, but it's no longer malaria that I torture myself with but you-know-what.

I am sure it all started when I found a lump in my breast last year. It turned out to be nothing, but the idea planted, the weed spread. I drove myself to the screening centre, nearly got trapped in the hospital car park (FFS) and cried when the radiologist said it was all OK. And now I check my breasts constantly, rush to have a smear test and examine strange little growths on my body obsessively. As my entire system begins to misfire codes, small lumps appear on my feet or the side of my nose. And I touch and wonder, fiddling with my new abnormalities like worry beads.

And obviously I don't go to the doctor. Because most of me knows it's a sugar hangover, or overtiredness or just little hormonal shifts that are causing these strange developments. Not cancer. And the stupid part lies in the knowledge that if it ever is cancer, all this worrying and fantasising won't make the dealing with it any easier. Same with worrying about burglaries. Beyond basic common sense (don't smoke 60 a day, don't leave doors open, etc.), is constant vigilance just a quality-of-life destroyer? It's certainly not the way to true peace of mind…

## Just Because You Are Frightened, Doesn't Mean You Are Not Brave

Do you feel cowardly sometimes? A bit less than? As though, if you were more of a person, with more backbone, more guts, more soul, more power, you would be living a nobler life? A braver life?

Do you feel frightened? Often? As though bad things are in the post? As though you don't have the wherewithal, the emotional muscle, the faith to carry on?

Let me tell you something now and forever: just because you are frightened, doesn't mean you aren't brave. You are truly brave. The more fearful you feel, the more heroic you are. You are carrying on. You are doing the best you can with the information you have at this time.

Even admitting to feeling scared is brave. At least you're feeling the feelings. We are at our worst when we try to power through, jet-propelled by grim determination and denial. Do that and you run out of road in the end. Do that and you stop blooming and start calcifying. Do that and you deny yourself the chance of any solace.

Fear is a message indicating danger. If you are too afraid, if the world is closing in on you, then the terror is a helpful indication that you need some help.

Never be ashamed of being frightened. Shame is the enemy of growth. Tell someone that you are panicking. They are probably panicking too. We are all fucking panicking. It's one of the reasons that we are wonder women.

## Chapter 2

# WHAT COULD POSSIBLY GO WRONG?

MEN MIGHT HAVE SEX ON THE BRAIN. But women have sex *in* the brain. We think about sex fewer times a minute, but we think about it for longer, and in more complicated, narrative ways – a detailed landscape involving not just a friendly penis but also clean, crisp sheets, a good hair day, expert kissing, rough and smooth, worship, degradation, complimentary words about our beauty and brilliance. We may be grown-up, but we never feel grown-up about sex. However many times we've done it, we never feel like we've nailed it. However old we are, we still think about it in the same fevered way that we did when we were teenage girls, our minds letting us go places (the guitarist from Duran Duran's bed, for instance) that our bodies would never reach. This powerful imaginative capacity might well be the thing that separates men from women.

Our sex brain is alive with a pulsing, amalgamation of moments, all the different fingertips and lips that have written on our bodies. It is a valuable storage facility. And just one of those moments (let's take five minutes with the personal trainer at that hotel in Turkey who was some kind of God and will henceforth be known as God) can keep us going for years. We make deposits in the sex-brain bank and we draw on them. The good ones never depreciate. They come and go.

And when we really have a crush on someone (they don't have to be someone we have actually met. They can be a character in a book, on television and, for one Midult, a long-deceased religious leader) these sex fantasies can become almost Versailles-like in their vast complexity and brilliance: lots of rooms, really great gilding, many flickering fireplaces, miles of moody corridor.

But they can betray us, these imaginary lovers and imaginary scenarios by virtue of their very imaginariness. Things are often better when they stay in our own heads. Like those arguments that we masterfully win in the shower. Because you never know until you try. Despite all our experience (oh, do stop going on) every new encounter involves a steeling of the mind, a 'Once more unto the breach'.

Imagine this – you have fancied someone for ages, gone to sleep thinking about them, imagined EVERYTHING not just the sex (but there is a lot of that), but also the doe-eyed look he gives you when he wakes up, how his skin smells, how hilarious he finds you. You *might* have got as far as practising your 'new' signature, a house, CHILDREN, and then back to the sex again. You have spent time and mental energy on this scenario, you have gone back to it again and again, filling it in, adding detail, colour and shade; it is a masterpiece. And then you are at a party, in actual real life, and he brushes his hand against your thigh in a way that definitely feels purposeful, and the imaginary and the real are finally meeting in some sort of space–time continuum mash-up that might actually destroy the universe.

Now your heads are moving closer together – are they? – they definitely are, and you are about to kiss – really? – you definitely are. And there it is, that sex-cruciating moment before any contact that is both the realisation of all the fantasy and also full of fear. Every encounter, every kiss, feels a little bit like this. A bit hot, a bit holy shit.

Then you start having sex…and it is nice enough, although halfway through you start wondering if you left your phone in the bar and would it be rude to ask him to stop for just a second while you go downstairs and check your handbag because, well, your life is in that phone and someone might have died? Or be dying? And you are missing the death. And there is no going back from that…This, by the way, was not part of the fantasy.

The female sex brain. It has great power but if we are honest we are still not completely sure how to control it. I mean yes, we know that we have the magic ability to keep relationships sexually alive for years through the muscle of our own imaginations. And we are not talking about role play, the horror of hearing a whispered 'tell me what you want' (Answer: £10 million pounds and to be left alone), or fishnets or firemen or mermaids or teachers or driving instructors or tennis coaches or nurses or aliens or nannies or policemen. But rather the ability of the sex brain to invite someone else to the party (quietly and discreetly and invisibly). They're there – Dylan from *Beverly Hills, 90210* or that barman from that wedding – but only you know they're there.

So far, so useful. But sex brains play tricks on us. We have flashbacks like a deranged junkie. One minute you are in a meeting listening to Geoff from Digital droning on about strategy, and suddenly there it is, the memory of a table pressing on your back, or a hand unhooking a bra or a tongue, and you are lost down that particular rabbit hole. 'I do apologise Geoff, could you repeat that?'

The sex brain is the reason that casual sex can be so emotionally dangerous. We are biologically programmed to release a bonding hormone that tries to find emotional resonance in what is essentially a physical act. Do not let yourself fall into the gap between the actual and the imagined. This takes concentration.

So yes, we should be a wary of our sex brains, but also proud of them; of their incredible focus and creativity and meandering ways. We will, after all, be spending more time with our imagination than we will with any man. And our imagination can always get it up.

# Five Guys You Probably Slept With

### 1. The One Who Was Completely In Love With You

Remember him? He sent you emails full of kisses, and maybe even handwritten letters, and he made you tea in bed but the sex was meh, and you wondered, 'Is this what love feels like?' While hoping…that it wasn't. You'd always imagined what it might be like to be adored but actually – get off me NOW.

### 2. The Hot One Who Looked Like He Was Engineered By NASA

Might have been a small-time sportsman or maybe a regional TV presenter who was really, really good-looking. Blindingly handsome. So good-looking that in photographs you look like Madge to his Dame Edna. So well built that he once bent over to feed the cat (not a euphemism) and your mum did an audible intake of breath. You have never forgiven her. Disgusting.

### 3. The Manic Depressive Who Gave Unbelievably Good Head

The moods were awful. He left you sitting in restaurants when he was depressed or just walked out of parties if you talked to anyone else. He kept you up all night when he was on a high: talking talking talking about the death of Princess Diana. But you had orgasm after orgasm after orgasm so put up with it as long as you could. About three months.

### 4. The Ugly One Who Was Mean To You

He clearly should have been GRATEFUL but, weirdly, he was not. It became about winning in the end. He ran off with your best friend. You can spin this however you want, but in no way did you win.

### 5. The Yucky One

Oh, you were Kate Moss and he was your Pete Doherty. In bad light, if you were squinting, he looked like Kurt Cobain. For the first time in your life you felt cool and wild and then, after six months of dating, woke up in the back of someone's car in Gloucestershire and he'd wet himself – and you. So you thought what the hell am I doing? And never saw him again. JOKE – you dated him for another year and a half. Oh God.

## Use It Or Lose It

Sex, when you haven't had it for years, is an odd prospect. People don't talk about this but for every Midult howling, 'Oh God, I haven't had sex in THREE MONTHS' there is a quieter Midult (sometimes single, other times married) thinking, 'I haven't had sex in five years. Will I ever have sex again? Possibly not. How do I feel about that?'

Because chasms open up; sexless ones. And the prettiest and perkiest of us fall into them. But when does a blip become a drought become a life sentence? And is there a way out/back/up?

So here's a bit of controversial advice from the front line: use it or lose it. You can cope with sex. You are an adult. You do not suffer the dramatics and the outrage of the 20-something on the 'You should be so lucky/I feel completely worthless/I am a goddess/I deserve nothing' roundabout of hell.

You are a grown-up and having sex will reconnect you with your species. Including the lows – but lose the lows and you lose the highs. Inconvenient truth.

Having sex helps you see life as a player (not a playa or even a *playa*) rather than an observer and that – in and of itself – is good for you.

Use it because otherwise – brace for an unfortunate turn of phrase – people will smell it on you. Metaphorically. And remember that you can always use it. You have never lost it. You just have to reconnect. Use Tinder. Use Bumble. Use the gym. Use role play. Whatever. Be safe. Don't quit. Also it's not true what they say about hymens growing back.

## 'How Many People Have You Slept With?'

We all have 'the list'. In my early twenties, especially during lean periods, I would occasionally go through it: the names, the numbers, which ones meant something, which meant nothing at all. I thought I would remember this list forever, I thought it was indelible, defining…But with age comes a generous and kindly blurring, and now I realise I can't remember all their names, or even how many there have been. And do you know what, it doesn't matter, it doesn't mean a thing, how many or how few. The list is not an alternative curriculum vitae, graded and scored, we are not meant to be judged on it. And we will not be judged on it (shall we say somewhere between 15 and 25? A couple of Bens, a couple of Marks, maybe?). Which is why 'How many people have you slept with?' is such a silly question. No one should ask it. And everybody lies except the weirdos. So here are comebacks should you find yourself asked:

1. 'I don't know, I don't have the spreadsheet on me.'
2. 'What? Including your brother? And your dad?'
3. 'Somewhere between nine and nineteen. Or ninety. There's definitely a nine involved. Or maybe a six. Hmmm…'
4. 'Does it have to include premature ejaculators and "put-ins"?'
5. 'More than Kate Middleton, less than Kate Moss.'
6. 'Fewer than Prince Harry, more than Prince William.'
7. 'Do you know when I can't sleep I count them, instead of sheep?'
8. 'Shall I show you, via the medium of mime?'
9. 'Do you mean men or women?'
10. 'I stopped counting at a hundred.'

# 10 Ways To Swerve A Hard On

Sometimes, if we're just not in the mood, we might:

1. Start a fight about his ex-girlfriend.
2. Say that someone has remarked that you look like his mother.
3. Set the smoke alarm off. Then the burglar alarm. Then the car alarm.
4. Start meditating.
5. Make demands you know will not be met: 'Only if you go bed linen shopping with me at John Lewis this weekend.'
6. Say you want a baby.
7. Put on an Adele record and start crying.
8. Start speaking in a Mrs. Doubtfire accent: 'Come over here now you big boy.'
9. Finally reveal the real number of people you've slept with…
10. Have hysterics every time you look at it.

# All Our Coital Concerns

### Pre-Coital Concerns
- Is my wax wonky? Because actually, I didn't have time to book a wax so I did a home Immac and, oh dear, it was dark and I was in a rush and is it straight or do I have a bent bush?
- Where the fuck is my good underwear? You know, that matching Coco de Mer set that I break out on special occasions? It's a bit tight and bulgy these days but still. So uncomfortable. Can I even remember how to put it on? Or take it off? Oh whatever, it's not the packaging that matters, right?

- What happens if I laugh? There's always the risk. Nerves, you know? But it can have a very deflating effect. Must not laugh. Must not…Oh God.
- Do I fake tan? I want to look like a honeyed Bardot but I do not want to smell like a cheap chocolate biscuit. *spends hours worrying about Bardot-to-biscuit ratio* Clearly am now starving.
- Can I really get the right amount of drunk? Just that little bit lubricated. Jolly. Tequila-tinted. Prosecco-perfect. Gin and juiced. Not falling over and suggesting a threesome with the neighbour and too numb to come. That would be bad.
- Is there life on other planets? Can courgetti ever really hit the spot? The mind wanders.

## Mid-Coital Concerns

- The damp patch. No not that one. The one on the ceiling. How damp is too damp? Will the ceiling fall in? The Earth is supposed to be moving, right?
- Why can't I focus on what's happening? Focus focus focus focus. Maybe I've got Adult Onset ADHD. Would that be AOADHD? Maybe I should start meditating again. What was that app called? The one with the sexy monk guy voice. Mmmm… sexy monks.
- Do I look OK? Do I seem OK? Is this angle OK? Am I behaving like a normal, human woman? Am I a normal, human woman?
- Shit! I forgot to put passata on the grocery order. That's my Bolognese buggered. Do you think I could stop this and then quickly add it on. It would only take a minute. Or might that seem a bit mad? I could just write it down because otherwise I will forget. Oh God I can't remember anything at the moment.
- Where is my phone? Where is my phone? WHERE IS MY PHONE?
- Oh God I need to phone my mother back. I haven't even listened to her voicemail. Why does she leave voicemails? Stop thinking about your mother. Stop thinking about your mother.
- This fitted bottom sheet feels like it's going to ping off. But really though, is it going to ping? I think it's ready to ping. It's pinging, it's pinging, it's…pinged. Sigh.

## Post-Coital Concerns

- How long do I have to lie here before I can go and put a wash on/get in a cab/check Tinder without looking insane/a bit cold-hearted/slutty?
- Why aren't I more daring? Why am I so vanilla? Is it too late to learn new skills?
- Is it safe to take my make-up off now or is he going turn the light on again?
- God I am thirsty, God I am hungry – is it too late to order a pizza?
- Did I just dislocate something? That click was not normal. And it almost, but not quite, hurts. Like my bone is humming or something.

- Am I too old to do what I just did?
- I want nice arms, I want nice arms, I want nice arms, I want nice arms.
- I really, really, really want to change the sheets now. NOW. But will that disrupt everything? (This feels a bit like when they change the tablecloth in the middle of dinner…)
- Does this mean I don't need to go to the gym this week? Five hundred calories just burnt – yesss.
- I wonder if they've got those nice kebab things at the butcher.
- Did he just say cock? I think he said cock. I can't believe he said cock. Who still says cock? Cock, cock, cock. Did I say pussy? Did I? I think. I. Did.
- I forgot to call my mother.
- Am I going to sleep? Please let me sleep. I can't deal with another sleepless night. I nearly ran over the cat yesterday and nearly sent the strategy report to the wrong Alan.
- Wait, hold on, AGAIN? Not poss.

## Do You Have Itchy Knickers?

Itchy knickers. It isn't a yeast infection, it's a state of mind and it means that you're… sniffing around. Persuadable. If you're single then it's a mission. If it strikes in the middle of a long-term relationship then care must be taken to ensure that irreparable mistakes are not made.

Itchy knickers make you wild-eyed and restless. They alter you pheromonally. They make you vulnerable to pastures new. People clock the change. Your friends say, 'How are you?' in a slightly more investigative way. People flirt with you their intention ramped up. Old male friends notice you. The only one who won't notice you and your itchy knickers is your partner. Maybe something's amiss. Or maybe the itchy knickers aren't personal and you need to just point those itchy knickers (and maybe knockers) in his direction and have sex every day for a month. Work it out of your damn system. Scratch those itchy knickers. And if they're still aflame? Well. Hmmm.

Take note of your itchy knickers. Knowledge is choice. You wear your itchy knickers; they do not wear you. And even if this warning is too late to heed, even if your itchy knickers have become greedy knickers, even if all hell has broken loose, at least when you overhear some woman whispering, 'I told you she had itchy knickers', you'll know what she's damn well talking about.

Itchy knickers. Turn them (not literally please) to your advantage. Sexual focus can make you powerful. Sexual incontinence? Please discuss.

## Am I Too Old For Party Sex?

So I've got two potentially frisky parties this Thursday followed by what promises to be an absolute humdinger on Saturday. A proper blowout. And so my question to you is not what to wear; is not what to drink; is not even what to say. My question to you is this: should I have a wax? Because maybe, just maybe, there might be an opportunity to get laid. Remember party sex? The sex you would never have had if you hadn't happened to be exactly that drunk at exactly that party?

Could it be that there is a 'victim' – I use that term in jest (no I don't) – just standing by the bar willing to get drunker than drunk and then slope off in a let's-pretend-we're-going-back-to-my-flat-to-talk kind of a way. Someone new. Fresh meat – I use this term in jest (no I don't) – who has never encountered me before and just…fancies a go. Of course, that man propping up the bar may be my future husband – I use that term in jest (actually I do – a triumph of experience over hope). There are no future husbands until perhaps one day, maybe, possibly, there is one. And then I could have party sex with him. For the rest of my life.

Equally, I may become so tequila-trigger-happy that I make one of those few and far between booty calls. To someone who will…tick the box. It never feels great after these (twice yearly) calls, but they are a thousand times easier than the self-loathing and misery that sits in for 24 hours after a bad date. Dates are risky. They can sting. Party sex is just…what it says on the tin.

## The First Shag: What Not To Do

1. Cry.
2. Laugh.
3. Roll your eyes.
4. Talk about food.
5. 'Let's take a selfie!'
6. 'I love you.'
7. 'What's your name again?'
8. 'THAT'S WHAT I'M TALKING ABOUT!'
9. 'Am I the best you've ever had?'
10. 'Shall I call you a cab?'
11. 'Oh well, maybe it'll be better next time.'
12. Ask him to empty the dishwasher.
13. Ask him to make you a sandwich.
14. Go to the bathroom and text him: 'Can you be gone by the time I come out?'

15. Make a phone call and describe exactly what just happened to your friend in front of him.
16. 'You seem familiar...Do you have a brother?'
17. 'You seem familiar...Do you look like your father?'
18. Immediately have a shower saying, 'Dirty girl, horrible, horrible, dirty girl.'
19. 'Well, that's an hour I'll never get back.'
20. 'Well, that's three minutes I'll never get back.'
21. 'Who was that incredibly handsome man you were talking to at dinner? Is he seeing anyone?'
22. 'Again. NOW!'
23. 'I just don't think this is going to work.'
24. 'So it's true. Losing your virginity is as grim as people say...'
25. 'The irony is, I think you'd really get on with my husband.'
26. Get out your vibrator and say, 'Some things need to be left to the professionals.'

## Casual Sex: Proceed With Caution

You won't know how you feel about casual sex unless you've tried it. It has its good points – you get to have sex, obviously, and not just maintenance sex, but sex you actually really want. Hot, reckless, this is a bit dirty and I love it sex. Not that you can't have all that with a partner – it's just there's none of that post-fuck chat about lunch with his mother at the weekend or who can be in for the grocery delivery tomorrow. Just wanting each other physically has its charms and when it works, casual sex can be very empowering. You're two adults taking what you want. It's selfish. And sexy.

But then there's a thing that makes it a bit complicated, as things tend to do. It's a hormone called oxytocin, released by a woman after sex and designed to make her feel trust and attachment. You know, because of babies and whatnot. That complicates things by the very nature of it being something instinctive and therefore slightly irrational. So if you do start to feel attached to your casual sex compatriot, the point is that it's completely normal. It's not clingy, it's science. Perhaps the way to not go mad is to know when to get out. Or when to be brave and suggest this could be a relationship after all.

Because actually, there is something courageous about casual sex. You're opening yourself up to all the emotional possibilities of being intimate with someone, even if you think you're not. Perhaps it's just as much about being honest with yourself about what you want. And if that turns out to be a rampant no-holds-barred sex-fest where he's dressed as Zorro and you are a lusty señorita who is having problems with her corset, then good for you.

# Sex Flashbacks

One minute you are minding your own business in a meeting or on your daily commute and next minute your brain has summoned an X-rated memory and you have a fucking flashback. Like...

### The First Orgasm
Remember that Israeli soldier on your gap year on a small beach in Thailand and you were a bit stoned and so completely shell-shocked afterwards that you just got up and left? And every now and then you are reminded of how that felt and go quite dizzy with it.

### The Pop-Up
Nothing livens up a supermarket shop like a sudden full-blown sex flashback, from that morning, or last week, or that time in the student union loos, and you do a full body blush and you are in the cereal aisle and you think, 'Everyone can tell I am thinking about sex right now.' Your hands are shaking. Are you having a hot flush? Is this the menopause?

### The Random Body Part
There you are on the Underground when an inner thigh, or a neck tuft, swims across your vision and whoosh you are there. You are not sure whose it was or at what point in the, er, proceedings it came into focus, but it's such a visceral memory you twitch a bit. At least it's not a smell. This time.

### The Who's That Girl?
Remember when you were working in Paris and you met a boy/man/whatever at a party and you left and spent *tout le weekend* shagging and smoking cigarettes and drinking red wine? Who was that girl? You think of her every so often. Was she happy?

### The Shaming Memory
Sometimes your mind will drag back a Neolithic memory that you really really don't want to remember – like that Australian guy you met in Earls Court and you all went out for drinks and then you snogged his much nicer friend but, and why you will never know, then went back and shagged the Aussie. And you still can't go to Earls Court without feeling the fear. You hate Earls Court. And Australians. You can't believe you are admitting this to yourself.

**The Just Before You Sleep Memory**
You are finally drifting off after an exemplary sleep hygiene session – no phones, no alcohol, no scary thrillers, only lavender and whale music – and suddenly you remember the IT guy. Please not the IT guy. You thought you'd performed a sexorcism on him. You hadn't. It remains a low point.

# Meet The M&S Penis

I saw some old girlfriends recently, we got drunk, stayed up late, the conversation inevitably turned to Penises We Had Known. It was so funny I may have slightly wet myself, particularly about the semi-famous artist who had got annoyed that my friend had never shown his penis enough 'respect'. The following night I was trying to explain this late-night conviviality to my husband. How nice it had been. I don't get to laugh like that so much these days, what with work and life.

'But you didn't talk about my penis did you?'

I paused. I mean, you must know this, boys? We do talk about your penises. They are not off-limits. They do not have a conversational *cordon sanitaire*.

'No, I mean, yeah, because it was, like, a chat about really awful penises that we had tried, and I was explaining how before I met you I had three really shit experiences: three really awful guys, each with really awful penises. Awful in different ways. There was the pencil penis: long and thin (he told me he was an internet millionaire, only had champagne in his fridge, bought books "by the yard" because they made him look clever and asked me to marry him before we'd even had sex). And then the thumb penis; so small I didn't even know it was in (he was wearing a trilby hat while he was at it. "Have you come?" I said. He had gone weirdly still. I had no clue what was going on down there). And then the one that was so wide I was worried I would never be able to get off it (he told me that he always liked to get to Glastonbury three days early, to meditate, do yoga, "set the place up, spiritually"). And then there was you, and your penis was just really nice. So that is all I said about your penis.'

Phew.

'Really nice. So you basically said I had an M&S penis.'

Silence.

He looked genuinely offended, like having a dependable high street penis was a bad thing. What did he want? Did he want to be billed as big and tough: a Land Rover penis? Or perhaps smooth and classy: a Ralph Lauren penis? Celebratory yet chilly: a Moët penis? Just a bit more upmarket: a Waitrose penis? Budget but big portions: the Lidl penis???

I mean there are worse things than M&S; we love M&S, especially the pants and the food. We can depend on it, we go to it when we are feeling a bit unsure of ourselves, when we don't want a challenge. No one really wants a challenging penis, especially not on a husband. So yes. This isn't just any penis. This is an M&S penis. And I married it.

## Where Can You Hide Your Vibrator?

If you have a cleaner, nosy friends, maybe a man-shaped presence in your life, possibly a child, a dog constantly truffling about for things to chew…If you have some or all of these things in your life, where the hell do you hide your vibrator?

1. In one of your old handbags. Until someone wants to play dress-up. Or you do a charity shop run and forget…
2. Behind the books on the bookshelf – until someone (else) decides to alphabetise them.
3. In your knicker drawer – where it will inevitably get tangled in a bra strap and fly out and hit someone on the nose when you are in a hurry one sweaty morning.
4. In the bottom of the weekly organic vegetable delivery box. No one ever delves down under the sprouting potatoes.
5. Round the back of the kitchen cupboard – the one where you have to reach around the corner and no one wants to because it's a bit spidery.
6. In the fish kettle. Stupid bloody thing.
7. In your wellies. Anyone fancy a walk? Oops.
8. In the Monopoly box. Hasn't been touched in…OH GOD CAN'T WE PLAY PICTIONARY INSTEAD???
9. Boot of the car. With the spare tyre and the anti-freeze. Until there's a breakdown. Yours.
10. In a box that used to contain a very tall bottle of bubble bath. In the hope that no one…helps themselves.

## Conversations You Have With Yourself During Sex

Me:         Good, I'm in the mood for this.
Also me:  Did I leave the iron on?
Me::        Raring to go. Let's have it!
Also me:  Because if I did, that's a real waste of electricity.
Me:         YES!
Also me:  And potentially extremely dangerous.
Me:         More. MORE.

Also me: Errr, can I smell burning?

Me: Weren't expecting THAT, were you!

Also me: No, wait – there's definitely something I forgot to do today?

Me: Yes, I am getting very good at this.

Also me: What day is it?

Me: Watch me place my leg over *there* like *that*.

Also me: Ah…the dry-cleaning!

Me: Bendy, bendy, bendy!

Also me: I've got nothing to wear to that party where my ex will be tomorrow.

Me: Going to stand up. Curveball.

Also me: And I forgot to pick up my anti-anxiety medication.

Me: Woooo!

Also me: Which means I'll turn up badly dressed AND insane.

Me: And…off the bed…onto the floor…hot.

Also me: OK, what the fucking fuck is that fucking mark on my carpet?

Me: Filthy carpet sex, YES!

Also me: If he has burnt a hole in my carpet, he is so dead.

Me: Taaaable…

Also me: How many times have I asked him not to smoke in the house?

Me: I am a goddess.

Also me: He does not listen to a single thing I say.

Me: He is also very good at this!!!

Also me: Selfish arsehole.

Me: I always like it when he does that.

Also me: I hate it when he does that.

Me: Gosh, this is a bit experimental.

Also me: Well he can go and check the iron in a minute as punishment for the carpet.

Me: LOVE THIS.

Also me: Could I get away with a micro-sleep?

Me: Just going to let go.

Also me: I mean, where am I going to be in ten years' time?

Me: LOVE HIM.

Also me: I wonder what my ten-years-from-now husband is like?

Me: Forever.

Also me: Hopefully he can get it up.

Me: I'm so lucky.

Also me: And has teeth and maybe a bit of hair.

Me: WAAAAAAA!!

Also me: WAAAAAAAA!!!
Me: That was amazing.
Also me: I hope he has a beard because I love beards.
Me: Need to pee.
Also me: Need to check Instagram.

## Too Full To...

I like food and I like sex. Indeed, I like a lot of food and a lot of sex. I am a woman of appetites. But not at the same time. I am not talking about someone attaching raspberries to my nipples, I am talking about those 'important romantic evenings', like Valentine's, like birthdays, like anniversaries, which always seem to involve a feastly amount of food SWIFTLY FOLLOWED by (what is meant to be) some emotionally resonant lovemaking. Who came up with this tautologous torture? Nibbles and then a multi-course fandango and flights of wine and OK yes let's have the cheese at the end, and a couple of chocolate bonbon things, and no, fennel tea is not going to make a dent in all that.

And now, now I am meant to want to have sex, to lie on my back (ouch, my tummy) and submit to more things being put into my body, when I am in a state of serious digestive shock, when I am numb (rather than frisky) with booze, when all I want to do is burp gently for a couple of hours. This, my fellow travellers, is called being 'Too Full to Fuck' and it is not really an excuse you are allowed to use, for some reasons to do with femininity and knowing not to have seconds.

But let's be realistic, no one expects you to have sex half an hour after Christmas lunch; children are often present, and there is *Doctor Who* on the TV, and there was bread sauce. Sex is for Christmas Eve and Santa costumes (sorry, maybe that's just me...). Can't the same division be applied to one's 10th anniversary celebrations and similar rituals. One night for eating, the following night for fasting and fucking. That way everyone is satisfied and no one gets indigestion.

## Does This Mean I'll Never Have Sex Again?

There are some things that I feel would significantly improve the quality of my life. They are neither expensive nor hard to find. And yet I resist. Because, if I succumb, I fear I shall never have sex again. And, from where I'm sitting, the odds don't need worsening. But I yearn for them. And some day soon I'll succumb to...

### Slippers
Not dainty ballet-shoe-shaped ones but chunky sheepskin and suede, buff coloured probably, contrasting very little with my grey and slightly scaly winter ankles. And maybe I won't get the more modern mule style but, instead, plump (plump being the operative word) for the almost wingéd moccasin style of old (old being the…). But then I'll flatten the backs with my cracked heels and they'll be mules anyway.

### Brushed Cotton Nightie
Preferably sprigged with flowers. Complete with Peter Pan collar. Hopefully a bit of smocking. Floor length with elastic around the wrists and then the most conservative of flounces. Basically a child's night dress but I'll be drinking vodka in it and anyone who wants to shag me wearing this would have serious sexual deviances. Like most of the people who want to shag me.

### Braces
Yes, many, many Midults are wearing braces to deal with the dreaded midlife snaggle-fang, but they are mostly partnered up. Imagine snogging someone for the first time with a mouthful of metal. Or coyly offering a blow job. I mean, they'd run screaming…

### Companion Pillow
Depressing name but it's not actually a fake boyfriend it's a V- or C- or S-shaped pillow to support my back. Actually, is that even more depressing?

### Arch-Supporting Insoles From Dr Scholl
I can feel my flat feet slapping against the floor, but imagine kicking your shoes off when things get steamy only for an arch support to fly out – so much worse than a chicken fillet in your bra. I might as well carry my sex toys in a tartan wheelie shopping trolley… (which I also quite want).

### Electric Blanket On One Side Only
Because you would, wouldn't you? Why get a big, electricity-guzzling one when I can get one just for…one. And turn it on when I want. And turn it off when I want. And never again have to worry about being cold and alone. I can be hot and alone.

## Welcome to Midulthood

# MIDULT MATHS

AT SCHOOL WE WERE NOT GOOD at maths, not good at all. 'It's not that you're bad at maths, it's just that you think you're bad at maths,' they said, which we thought was silly at the time. But with age comes an unexpected aptitude for mental arithmetic. Turns out we are boffins when it comes to certain strains of maths; the kinds of equations that relate directly to the mysteries of the Midult universe.

## Death Maths

Let's start with the dark sums: the balancing of mortality figures. The numbers are rarely resolved but constantly recalibrated according to aches, pains, missed smear tests, headaches, moles, sick friends, scaremongering headlines, cigarettes and birthdays. 'More or less than halfway through?' becomes the question as we throw our minds towards the big balance sheet in the sky.

## Alcohol Maths

The little getting-ready sharpener must be included in the evening's full mathematical reckoning as it may be the drink that tips the equation into something non-computable. The booze formula can only hold true if the number of units is equal to the number of waters, and if the units are crossbred then there is likely to be extreme malfunction. If cigarettes are introduced then the figures will not add up. Repeat, will not add up. Also, see death maths.

## Heartbreak Maths

This theorem operates around a system of constantly shifting risk analysis. For the mathematician mid-heartbreak, the calculation revolves around the scientific probability of actual survival. Once recovery is established as a viable option then the advanced numericist may be able to work towards an anti-bitterness formula. The single mathematician, embarking on an untested unknown, may or may not notice their subconscious performing an is-this-going-to-be-another-fucking-disaster computation. We become the romantic hadron collider seeking the perfect partner particle.

## Battery Maths

Remember a time before smartphones, when your battery would last three days? And you only panicked at 6 per cent. Nowadays it must not be less than 92 per cent charged upon leaving the house in the morning and all windows must be closed except for the one in use. If we are out all day then there will be NO listening to music or podcasts (I mean, are you insane? That takes us to 66 per cent in seven minutes) and easy on the Insta scroll. Ration it to one per hour. If the battery is lower than 50 per cent by midday (it always is) then activate humble charger-begging to ensure that it is over 70 per cent by early afternoon. Rookie error to think that anything less will see you through to home time. A frugal early afternoon opens a window for some Amazon action around the 4pm slump and full-on texting frenzy during the commute home. If you are the type who carries around one of those portable chargers, then you are not our people. (But can we borrow it, please?)

## Sleep Maths

If it's 9.30 now and you're on the main course, then you should be away by 10.30, which means home by 11, bed by 11.20 and lights off at 11.30 (as long as you don't decide to read the entire internet before you attempt to drift off), which means you might make it through to 5.30 and that's not a disaster. This is the crazy world of sleep maths. Forget the mysteries of the universe, sleep maths is the constant calculation ticking through our brains. Let's put Brian Cox on it and see if he can do something squiggly to time – is it linear? Is it quantum? We are far, far, far too tired to care. And, for a laugh, let's chuck jet lag into the equation to really mess with the equations.

## Wax Maths

So let's imagine a hot date happens. And you might decide to go in guns blazing and take what you want or you might decide to wait. 'Let's just wait…' We do not judge. That is the point of us. But, hang on, the next hot date is ten days away (he's travelling… or something) by which time the 'area' is all lumpy and bumpy and itchy and ragged but not yet ready for a re-wax no matter how much you exfoliate. The same, by the way (just to de-perv for a mo), is true of a two-week holiday. Day one = immaculate. Day 13 = slightly grizzled = sarong time.

## Caffeine Maths

This calculation is an exact science aiming to hit the perfect equilibrium between corpse and fiend. The baseline must be a comprehensive understanding of the subject's individual reaction to coffee at all times of the day and with and without other sustenance. We all know that three single shot coffees and no breakfast makes for a dynamically productive morning during which people will hide behind any available object – or even each other – to avoid contact with us.

## Pee Maths

It's the problem you wrestle with, for example, when you are making a cup of tea: do you wait for the kettle to boil and then pour the water or do you quickly run to the loo? But that's just the tip of the pee-berg. You will have probably bought a jumpsuit over the last couple of years. Now you have to throw that into the equation. (Especially if the jumpsuit unzips at the back.) Time spent undoing jumpsuit + urgency + distance to the bathroom = possible disaster. And the cut-off point for fluids at night. That's a whole Russell Crowe in *A Beautiful Mind* situation of its own: should I have this sleepy tea while watching the news? How about water? Just a sip. It's 9pm. Aarrrgghhh. If I have this now, will I wake up at 2am? 3am? Or push right through until 4am?

## Clothes Maths

OK. So. I really feel like wearing that shirt but I have to save it for that thing in two days' time so that leaves this shirt, which means I have to take off this skirt (as the colours are all wrong) and change my bra so there is no gaping and wear those trousers except the boots that go with those trousers are too high for the schlep I need to do this afternoon so it's the other black trousers but that means I have to change my knickers and actually this shirt doesn't go with them so I'll wear my Old Faithful dress with a different bra and Adidas Superstars and I've got some heels at the office but I've just realised that the coat that goes with Old Faithful doesn't go with the bag that I've left by the front door which means…CONTENTS TRANSFER ALERT. And that's today's maths done.

## Chapter 3

# DOES THIS STRAITJACKET MAKE ME LOOK FAT?

OUR BODIES HAVE THEIR OWN stories to tell. The people they've seen and the places they've been. And these tales – with their plot twists and their mini-triumphs and losses – have little to do with 'pretty'. After all, until I was about 40, I didn't really get to decide what pretty was. That was the men's job: boys at school, idiots at university, my father (lose weight and get your eyebrows looked at, he said), actors in films, male characters in books, guitarists in bands, model scouts, magazine editors, fashion designers. What they found attractive was what mattered. It mattered more than anything.

If we were rational beings who did not invest everything, even cushions and handbags, with emotional value, we would understand that our bodies are functional things, bones clad in muscle and fascia, all wrapped up in a permeable cladding of skin. A brilliant, clever and complex machine which also happens to contain things that are harder to dissect – mind, spirit, instinct, soul.

But we are not rational. We invest cushions and handbags with emotional value. Which means that when we look at our bodies, our faces, our eyes, our hair, our lips, we see so much more than function. We see two millennia of (mostly male) ideas about female beauty, fuckability, loveability and therefore worth. These are the criteria on which we judge ourselves physically, especially when we are young. Criteria based on the desires of people who don't even know us.

I remember when I first started looking at myself, really looking at myself. I was about 13 years old; that terrifying almost-woman age. The large mirror in my childhood bedroom also happened to have a picture of Marilyn Monroe – black and white, pixelated, overlaid onto the mirror, with just a small clear triangle in the corner for me. I would look at myself and think, 'Am I pretty?' with Marilyn Monroe looking back at me, showing me what pretty really was. So I started putting on make-up, lots of it, pale, matte foundation, glassy beige lip gloss, heavy black eyebrows, too much mascara. I was not planning on seeing anyone, this was just for practice, an experiment to help me answer the question. Am I pretty?

And I was not the one looking at me. When I looked at myself I was imagining what other people (boys) would see when they looked at me, with my chubby cheeks and my badly coloured in, heart-shaped lips and the skin that I thought was too rosy but I now see was perfect – even with its pimples.

It is no wonder I was disappointed by what I saw. And I felt that disappointment in my bones: not pretty enough, not thin enough, not the girl that gets chosen, not the girl who turns heads. Me and my lot developed a way of looking at ourselves where we would always lose.

We appraised ourselves by comparisons with other women. Not the woman sitting next to us on the bus, but models, actresses, people who are freaks because they are unusually symmetrical, people whose job it is to be looked at, people who are more often than not destroyed by their beauty. All those women who are so beautiful that they get turned into objects, which makes them so easy to break.

It is a bizarre dawning when we realise that exceptional beauty is not always a blessing. That the people we want to desire us and cherish us might not care about cheekbones and six packs. That sexy isn't about pouty lips and hair twiddling. If a potential lover wants only models then his libido may be linked to his ego in a dangerous, chilly and profoundly unerotic way.

As we grow we come into focus, we start seeing ourselves. We learn to think, 'What do I find beautiful?' Seeing our stories. Looking at our bodies with more curiosity than panic. It's not fun, losing the elasticity, but it is kind of interesting. Age, experience, wisdom, being a bit loved now and again, all help with that. It is very lovely to care less and less what other people think of your looks. To want to please yourself.

The mirror tells a different story these days. One which Marilyn Monroe is not part of. We see the accumulated scars from smiling too much, frowning too much, caring too much; speckled-egg blobs on the sides of our cheeks from sunbathing too much. Giggle crinkles. The beginnings of a wibbly neck. We see beauty that is not defined by anyone else. And flaws that matter if you let them. We no longer have bodies we had at 20. And, thank God, we don't have the brains we had at 20 either. We have what we have. We have ourselves.

## 10 Things Midults Do When They Look In The Mirror

1. Pulling the skin taut around the cheekbones. Gently, kindly, lifting the skin and thinking, 'I wonder what it would be like if I had a facelift, or a brow lift at least, or a bit of filler but of course I wouldn't but doesn't that make my nose look nobler, and look at my nasolabial lines and I can't believe I've thought the word nasolabial.'
2. Pigmentation examination. Find worst mirror. Ramp up the strip lighting (maybe find a head torch). Touch nose to glass. Allow eyes to refocus. Examine funny patches of colour all over your face.
3. Jawline prod. Not a prod, rather just applying a little pressure to the jaw. Firm. Like when we squeeze an avocado. Checking for what exactly? Flimflam that's what.

Loss of…the will to carry on.

4.  Chin hair inspection. You can feel the little fucker so why can't you see him? For once you've got tweezers to hand and you're not just 'worrying' the stubble with your middle finger. But you can't see it. Can it be blonde? Oh dear Jesus it's grey isn't it? A grey chin hair that evades capture.

5.  Teeth check. Is there anything stuck in your teeth? There is always stuff stuck in your teeth. And why are they going so snaggly? Braces? Just on the bottom? Yes. Braces. It's all the rage. You wonder how much they cost.

6.  Turning head slowly from side to side. This way you can fully inspect your chicken neck. And how much, er, definition there is left between jaw and neck. Stretch a bit. A bit more…

7.  And then stroking that bit between your neck and chin. Is it getting bigger? Is it getting flabbier?

8.  Raising eyebrows and then seeing how quickly the creases go back on your eyelids. Maybe you'll start timing it.

9.  Shooting yourself a winning smile – you know the kind: super-dynamic, irresistible, there's practically a twinkle. Ting.

10. Wave at yourself (both hands) and quietly watch your arms flap in the breeze.

# Are You Snaccident-Prone?

What is a snaccident? It's the act of eating by mistake. 'Just an innocent mistake, your honour. I was basically a bystander.' Turns out, life is just one big snaccident waiting to happen. Like Easter or Christmas or Mondays…

### The Bread Herring

This is a nice restaurant. So much to look forward to. No, we don't need bread thank you. Oh really? Homemade? Well, just put it there, I won't touch it. And anyway as I was saying, he just wants me to dress up as a – wow, that's good, with the salty butter. Just a nibble because I am pretty much completely gluten-intolerant and…do you have any more of the nutty one?

### Deliverwrong

Need to be healthy tonight. You know, just low-level anorexic, because of that dress I want to get into and there's only toast in the cupboard and that would be unhealthy so I think I'll order in. Just to avoid chomping on Crunchy Nuts at 11pm. Maybe some Lebanese. Just grilled chicken. And salad (the one with the fried bread bits because it's pretty much the only one they do) and then hummus. Always hummus. And moutabal.

Don't know how to pronounce it, do know how to eat it. And those pastry things stuffed with healthy spinach. And cheese. And isn't baklava made with healthy honey?

### Fill-Your-Facebook

Late at night. Feeling low. Everyone is asleep. You are deep-diving into pictures of your ex and chomping to assuage that odd feeling of regret.

### The Eater-Egg Hunt

It's for the kids! Isn't this fun? All for the kids! Not for us! Look at those tiny shiny balls of chocolate. Weeny little things that can do no harm. Oval-shaped innocence. Just one. Darling, shall I hold your basket for you? *stands behind large bush* Darling, that naughty squirrel ate some of your eggs. Bad squirrel.

### Hangover-Doing-It

The acid, the acid, the acid. I'll have a smoothie. Just a smoothie. Something light. More of a snack than breakfast because breakfast food. Oh God no. Eggs? Never again. Porridge? Leave now and never darken my door. Pasta? Yes, pasta. Pasta is what my body needs and I must listen to my body. So, 50g of pasta for one person it says? Well, I'm eating for me and for the devil in my tummy and the demon in my head. Pasta and cheese.

### The Snacado

Because one time you were doing the Ocado shop super-fast and you uncharacteristically decided that you needed Dairy Milk, and you didn't look at the grams because you are so busy and when it arrived it was the 360g one, which is practically the size of a sheet of A4, and it went. And since then it's always on your favourites and you are always 'forgetting' to reduce the size because you know, you are so busy.

### The Netflix And Chomp

Nothing goes better with some incredibly harrowing homicidal thriller than salt and vinegar Kettle Chips, and oh the dishwasher is on so there are no clean bowls, so we'll just open a family-sized packet, and oh great they've just murdered and dismembered another woman, and oh hell the crisps are finished.

### Air-Portly

Just as you can't get pregnant when you have sex standing up, calories don't count at the airport. Airport calories are like Monopoly money. So I'll have that one club sandwich and then I'll buy one for the plane with a flapjack and also dark chocolate because dark chocolate is good for me and that dried fruit sharing bag (I am travelling alone) is full of vital nutrients that the recycled aeroplane air might somehow rob me of. I need to pick up some family-sized Skittles (have I mentioned I am travelling alone?) to suck so that my ears don't hurt and is that a Burger King?

### Canap-Ig
Well, I probably won't have dinner and I don't want to be drunk too quickly and I certainly need to mop up the champagne breath and better get two of those blinis before they go past. Now I've got smoked salmon breath, which is clearly a disaster, so...cocktail sausage? Oh dear, now I've unleashed hell because who can eat just one cocktail sausage? That's not normal. Six is normal. Yes I'd love to join you guys for dinner. Pizza? Perfection. Starving.

### Comfort Tweating
Something has happened. A terrible election result or the death of a teen idol. Then you start worrying about the Queen and David Attenborough. There's nothing for it but toast.

### Legs, Bum And In Your Tums
My metabolism is an *inferno*. My muscles are *pillaging* their way through fat. I have earned a hot cross bun and a sausage roll and the trainer said that the HIIT session would keep burning energy for 24 hours so, presumably, that is a pink ticket…

## Whose Body Is This Anyway?

Most of the time, my body is my body. But then, a few days a month, it stops being just my body and becomes a random selection of flesh Lego, none of it fitting together properly. Working in parallel to this is my wardrobe. Most of the time my wardrobe is full of clothes – far from ideal but generally workable. But then, a few days a month, it becomes a portal to horror, disgust and despair.

PMT, be it of the adolescent or perimenopausal variety, does not merely wreak havoc on mood (fuck the lot of you and the horse you rode in on, by the way), it also volcanically disrupts the way we feel about our physical selves. Even if we have learnt to be accepting (or embracing) of the many flaws, a dollop of hormones renders us hopeless. Getting dressed for work in the morning becomes an almost unassailable mountain. Nothing works. We don't work. Our bodies don't work. Our lives don't work. Total malfunction.

And it's not to do with fatness. Yes, we swell a little and ache a little and bloat a bit.

There may be chin spots and disobedient hair. It's to do with wrongness. Our bodies no longer fit us. We are revolting. It is extreme enough for us to feel truly altered but subtle enough for us to know that people will only see ugliness. 'When did she get so ugly? So ungainly? So utterly unlovely?'

And we never get philosophical about this. Even if we have the circumspection to glance at a diary or period app; even if we hold the rhythm of our cycles in our heads. Life, as we know it, is over. We do not deserve to be seen. Until next week.

## Things That Were Diet Foods In The Nineties

1. Porridge. Vast vats of it. Made with semi-skimmed milk. And honey. Then a bit more honey. And some banana because it's fruit and I need energy because of the workout I nearly did this morning. Porridge at desk at 9.30. Vastly expanded stomach capacity. Ravenous by 11.

2. Jacket potatoes. The skin is pure fibre apparently. And it's a (large) vegetable. No, I won't have cheese because that's a bit fattening so I'll just have that tuna mayonnaise instead. Yes please, butter would be good. Bit more? Mashed in? No, I won't have salad. It will make me too full and I have a party to go to tonight.

3. Sushi. The rice bowls count as sushi because they come from the same kitchen as the lean tuna sashimi, right? Of course right. And one of those noodly-doodly soups on the side. Do you even know how good this pickled ginger is for your metabolism? Like, so good.

4. Brown pasta, brown rice, brown toast, brown anything. You can eat literally as much of it as you like so long as it's brown. Might as well be lettuce.

5. Lattes. I'll just have three of these coffees and I won't have breakfast. No solids. Does this mean I've got an eating disorder?

6. Hummus with pitta bread. I'm basically on the Mediterranean diet, skipping through olive groves, which means I'll not only live until I'm a hundred but I'll look like Sophia Loren in about five minutes. Such good OILS in hummus.

7. Sugar-free sweets. An entire food group if I can just ignore the effect Sorbitol has on my tummy. Oh God. Back in a minute…

8. Diet Coke. As in 'Can I have a Big Mac meal and a Diet Coke?' Because the Diet Coke will make it ALL GO AWAY.

9. Baked crisps.

10. Juice. We now know that juice is basically a Mars Bar in a glass. AKA Satan's sperm.

# Hair Today, Hair Tomorrow

One minute you are a normal, functioning human woman. You practise safe hair removal, armed with a Venus razor and easy access to a professional waxer. And then all of a sudden you are not a run-of-the-mill adult woman, you are Chewbacca. Hair here. And here, and here. Wiry ones. It is a case of constant vigilance because, what would happen if you just let them grow wild and free? Nothing good.

### Chin

I am nothing without moisturiser. I moisturise therefore I am. I am dewy, like spring. Despite the booze and the coffee and occasional menthol cigarette, my skin is a temple. During a furtive office moisturise I suddenly connect with a stubborn foreign thing on my chin. THIS HAPPENS ALMOST EVERY DAY. I no longer leave the house without tweezers.

### Small Of Back

Nothing sexier than that rogue hair springing from the small of my back. That I can feel catching on my knickers but through some twist of terrible fate keeps evading my attempts at removing it. Something to do with the angle. Hold on…And then I catch myself in the bathroom mirror doing this contortion. Back fat. Loss of dignity. *passes out*

### Knee

Not just a light hairy leg but a full-grown black hobbit crop. There on the knee cap. With lots of hobbity friends. Can you see it through the tights? Do I shave it? Will it come back thicker? Should I just give up and draw a face on my knee and give it a name?

### Neck

There I am doing some sweeping, upwards cleansing movements that a facialist once told me to do in my twenties, when, what fresh hair is this? NOOOOOOOO. Neck hair. Soft goaty tufts. But brown. Dark brown. Sweet, really. And also disturbing.

### Boobs/Chest

It's the hormones. The hairmones. It's the living end. A black boobic hair. And when they said 'This'll put hairs on our chest' I didn't BELIEVE them. It's all a terrible trap.

# Fitness Fiascos

However virtuous we feel, however golden our intentions, however committed our regimes, truly terrible things can happen in Lycra.

1.  That time you became convinced that the bearded guy who was always on the cross trainer when you were doing weight work was someone from Coldplay. Is this not the perfect man – a rock star that no one recognises? You tried to marry him for three months. He never once looked up from his cross trainer.
2.  That time when you became so psychotically territorial over the second from the left in the bank of six running machines that you asked someone to swap when you found them on it. They pretended not to hear you through their headphones.
3.  That time when you were in downward dog and realised that a hugely famous actress was behind you. The rest of the class was a waste of time – then you tried to follow her into the shower, which was not good for anyone.
4.  That time you moved a towel out of the way with your foot to make way for your yoga mat, thinking it had been left by the class before, and a cross woman crossly hissed, 'You kicked my towel!!!' And namaste to you too.
5.  The time one teacher said, 'If you can control your anus, you can control your mind,' and you and your friend laughed for the remaining 43 minutes.
6.  When the personal trainer at the induction to your new gym was so handsome you could barely look at him, and you were not concentrating, and when he admired your athleticism you knew you were being played but you didn't mind and instead you giggled, and you swear someone snorted. Excruciating.
7.  But not as embarrassing as when you had to ask him how to turn the running machine on ten minutes later.
8.  That time you fanny farted in the hip yoga place. You still can't believe it. *stares into the Midult distance*
9.  That time you decided that couples who run together have fun together except it really wasn't fun and you are very much no longer together. In fact, you fucking hate each other and he runs like a girl. Fast though. Fuck him and his weird foot-glove trainers.
10.  That time you wore your poshest athleisurewear to 'brunch' at that Australian 'brunch' gaff and, when you bent over to pick up your handbag, THEY SPLIT. And the ladies in there were not the laughing/warm/sympathetic kind.

# All The Diets We've Done

Diets are bad. Diets make you fat, mad or a bore. Often all three. You know. You've been on a lot of diets. Some real, some imaginary, some accidental. You've lost stones and put them back on again through various nefarious methods including:

**The Backpack Diet**
You went to India. When you came back your mum picked you up from the airport and cried. The one time in your life that you've been 'worryingly thin', which is always the aim.

**The Cabbage Soup Diet**
You bought a flask in John Lewis. You stayed at your best friend's house because you were doing this together. You boiled the cabbage and you braced yourself for the week ahead. The weird bit of the diet when you were allowed to eat half a baked potato is still the best gastronomic experience of your life.

**The Atkins Diet**
Anna Wintour had steak for breakfast and so did you. You had bad breath, a bad attitude and bad skin. You were so angry that you had bacon coming out of your pores. Wow that weight came back fast.

**The Only Eating Sashimi Diet**
You only ate sashimi. Pre-huge-party. By the time the party came you were skeletal and dead behind the eyes and the dress you had bought didn't fit and you went home at 8.30pm alone.

**The No Carbs After 10am Not Much Besides Diet**
At first it was great and you had cake for breakfast: 'Look at me it's 9am.' A stone and a half that you didn't really need to lose just went. And then your mind went. When you went to the doctor to tell him about your anxiety attacks he was very annoyed by your eating lunacy.

**The 5:2**
You have never ever been so obsessed with food as you were on the two days a week of 500 calories. 'It's easy!' they cried. You got fat.

### The Broken Heart Diet

You didn't mean to but you just melted. You have never looked hotter or been sadder. If you had a choice you would always be fatter and happier. The rule of thumb is that a happy balance is about a stone heavier than you were at your most miserable.

# Naked Locker Room Behaviour

### The Naked Group

The ones of all ages who congregate in the sauna to chat and sweat and talk about the roadworks on the M25 that are driving everyone mad and whether democracy is dying – but naked.

### The Back-Turner

The one who will discreetly turn her back on you as you get changed or as she gets changed in case anyone feels awkward about the nakedness or you wrongly feel she is looking at your boobs (she would never look at your boobs).

### The Topless Hair Dryer

The one who takes a long time drying her hair – but with only her bottom-half clothed and her boobs out like this is her own private space. You actually really admire her.

### The Shy Dresser

The one who tries to get dressed with a towel wrapped round her so no one sees an inch of flesh. It takes her twice as long than if she just threw caution to the wind and freed the nipple.

### The Solitary Nude Wanderer

The one who drifts about the changing room for no apparent reason with a massive untamed bush. She might let it dry naturally, she might give it a quick blast with the hairdryer. But she'll always end up putting herself into all kinds of nothing-left-to-the-imagination positions while she applies body moisturiser.

### The Confident Pensioner

The one who is definitely over 70 and has moved into that very healthy headspace where she could not care less about anyone's nakedness, let alone her own. She'll happily listen to a story about someone else's grandson as she slaps clouds of talc under each arm and lets it all gloriously hang out.

**The Excessive Talker**
The one who sits naked in front of your locker, staring at themselves in the mirror and talking very loudly on their mobile phone: 'So I said to him, "We're only going on one skiing holiday this year, do not push me, Ambrose."' / 'Did you see what she was wearing? Who does she think she is, Cher or something?' / 'It's not a party wall! How many more times do I have to explain this??'

**The Stunner**
The naked one with the incredible body who you can't help staring at because they're in such great shape.

## Conversations You Have With Yourself In The Gym

Me:        Good to be here.
Also me:   What in the bastard hell am I doing here?
Me:        Good to be looking after myself.
Also me:   I want a big drink.
Me:        Gonna warm up first…
Also me:   I have no idea how to work this…
Me:        Look at me, I'm jogging!
Also me:   I'm going to be sick.
Me:        Wow, I managed five minutes – I'm fitter than I thought.
Also me:   Someone call an ambulance.
Me:        OK, what next?
Also me:   I need to lie down.
Me:        The cross trainer…
Also me:   No idea which one that is.
Me:        To work on my…glutes?
Also me:   The only muscle group I can remember the name of.
Me:        The setting the trainer suggested is much too high.
Also me:   Get me off. GET ME OFF.
Me:        I need something to work towards, surely?
Also me:   Like my own death.
Me:        Good to get a sweat going.
Also me:   Oh God, am I ugly-sweating?
Me:        Feels like something is happening.
Also me:   Is my face angry-red?
Me:        Buns of steel, buns of steel.

Also me: I can't even see my own arse – why am I doing this??

Me: Going to do the pulling thing with weights now.

Also me: I want a cheeseburger and a nap.

Me: Strong arms like Madonna.

Also me: To push away all those 22-year-olds who want to go out with me.

Me: OK, this is…

Also me: Boring/horrendous/pointless/evil…

Me: …quite hard work.

Also me: Now can't feel my hands.

Me: Right. Abs.

Also me: (laughing) I mean, what abs?

Me: Core strength is everything.

Also me: Core strength is Spanx.

Me: Feeling strong.

Also me: These are the never-before-seen-deep-sea-fish in *Blue Planet II* of muscles.

Me: Keep going…

Also me: These muscles don't have names.

Me: Tired, but good.

Also me: No pulse. Dead.

Me: Stretch…

Also me: Stretcher.

## Welcome to Midulthood

# SOME MIDULT URBAN MYTHS

Ladies, wherever you are, if you exist, we salute you.

## The Lottery Winner
She just had one shiny two-pound coin in her pocket. She'd never played the lottery before, but hey, she thought, 'I'll buy a ticket', and BOOM she won five million quid, paid off her mortgage, bought all of Ganni and headed off on a Midult gap life.

## The Person Who Is Married To Someone They Met On Tinder
Oh, you know so-and-so who's a friend of so-and-so's? Anyway his sister's cousin met someone on Tinder and they are getting married in Capri this year. So romantic. This story somehow neutralises all of the hopelessness, like a sexual encounter Etch A Sketch. Enough for you to keep swiping, in a totally dispirited fashion.

## The Woman Who Put On Three Stone And Became Unprecedently Happy In Her Own Skin
There we are constantly wondering how many biscuits is too many biscuits and there she is, this mythical creature who is just happy with her weight and whose husband has never fancied her more. No more looking back at pictures from 20 years ago and cursing herself for thinking she was fat then. Someone, somewhere is having all the bread and all the sex.

## The Woman Who Didn't Wake Up Just Before The Orgasm In Her Dream
Listen, there must be a woman out there who manages it, is able not to wake up just at the start of the best orgasm of both her waking and subconscious lives. Reinforces the possibility of a happy ending.

## The Woman Who Let Her Hair Go Grey And Has Never Looked Younger
Not the woman who hasn't had time to get her roots done and is looking a bit wild, like she's coming undone. Not the woman who is experimenting with a silver wash in a baby-step way to transitioning to grey. Not the woman who has a root wand that is not really working out for her. No, this woman went grey and is suddenly an Instagram influencer with a million followers and a shampoo deal with L'Oréal. DO NOT TRY THIS AT HOME.

## The Woman Who Had A Brilliantly Life-Changing Idea In The Middle Of The Night, Didn't Write It Down And Remembered It The Next Morning
Only joking.

## Chapter 4

# IF IT AIN'T BROKE

## (but it probably is)

STUFF IS ONLY STUFF, RIGHT? Things are only things. So why do I get a dollop of calm every time I open the doors to the linen cupboard? Why do the fresh, folded towels and ironed sheets make me feel a tiny bit saner? And why, seeing as stuff is only stuff, do I feel so much more in touch with myself, peaceful even, when I walk through the front door and see a nice mirror, a pretty rug, all chosen by me, all in their proper place? The home that I have built myself is a place of charm and order, it is what I would like my brain to look like, if I had the option to start from scratch and get the decorators in – tidy, warm, fragrant, with flattering lighting, no surprises, and lots of little presents, given to me, by me.

At home I am surrounded by acts of generosity to myself. I didn't need that pink Murano vase but I love it. I could have walked past that chair, but I bought it. Even though it is lemon yellow velvet. These are pockets of self-pleasure, simple, not indulgent or spoilt, and actually quite necessary if we are going to talk about equilibrium. But I have had to learn how to give myself presents, to stop waiting for someone (a man, a parent) to give them to me. That didn't come naturally and no one taught me that it was OK.

When my mother was a 'girl' she wasn't allowed to be generous to herself. Nice things were bought for her, not by her. She never even went out to dinner with another girl. It wasn't done. Women had to wait for a man to ask them out to dinner. Hot new show? Tough luck babes – where is the man to buy the tickets, be the escort and prove unsafe in taxis? Nowadays we can have dinner with whoever we want. Or – deep breath – alone. Nowadays we can have a baby alone. Our lives, our money, our bodies, our choices. So if we don't wait for dinner and we don't wait for marriage then why wait for stuff? The good stuff. The stuff that is usually bestowed rather than bought? The jewellery. The art. The heirlooms.

A couple of years ago I had a bit of cash saved up and I knew that I wouldn't have any cash for years to come (that proved viciously true), mostly because I was single and pregnant. I felt I deserved a love token. From myself, to myself. So – even though I was moving house, kitting myself out for an impending baby, panicking, I bought myself a watch. I wear it every single day and I am thrilled that I delivered it to myself. So I feel qualified to say: buy yourself a present. Might be that a KitchenAid will make you happy. Could be a memory-making holiday. Or a diamond. I'm not talking shopping addict credit card debt. I'm talking about that window of solvency when you can reward yourself.

Part of coinciding with yourself means losing interest in the disposable: single-use plastic, non-nutritious people, life's dust-collectors. So, even though we all feel we should be chanting that tired old 'stuff is only stuff' mantra, let us recognise that stuff can be resonant with meaning, with experience, with wisdom. It can sing with comfort, beauty, practicality and memory. Stuff is how I feather my nest. So that I can be still. Still and content – with my rug, my chair, my lamps, my choices, my life.

## Property Porn

If you were to open our laptops and type in our passwords you would find porn. It would quickly become clear that we have a problem with porn. Porn that dulls the senses. Porn that bleaches reality and makes human encounters less rich. Porn that makes you question what you have and what you want and whether anything you have genuine access to will ever be exciting enough. Exotic porn. Domestic porn. Porn.

No word of a lie; we are obsessed. And our search terms entirely depend on our state of mind at any given moment. Do we hope to feel humiliated, subjugated, appalled or inspired, powerful and all-conquering? Welcome to the bleak world of property porn. Insidious, addictive, property porn: the highway to dissatisfaction and self-loathing.

On an optimistic day, we look at houses that cost many times more than our properties would sell for. We visualise a remarkable financial year, the ability to upgrade while absorbing stamp duty into the equation and simultaneously reducing mortgage payments. The area is a little less 'real'; the kitchen a vast, elegant cooking/sitting/sprawling situation; there is a dressing room (imagine that). There is a spare, spare bedroom that has 'gym' written all over it because the at-home office can be in the shed at the end of the (non-overlooked) garden. All this is in London (Zones 1 and 2 only) by the way – if we are talking rural porn then hand us that *Country Life* and let us examine those semi-statelies. Party barn anyone? Pottery studio? Ping pong room? Staff cottage? Hammam? Some days – those days when anything seems possible – we type 'no max price' into the search bar and really roll around in the mud.

On less confident days we look at flats for half the price of our current homes. Just in case. Occasionally we experiment with a vast, tumbledown Bordeaux chateau or a rambling Hebridean farmhouse, but mostly it's grubby places within a five-mile radius of where we sit.

This kind of porn reflects how we feel about our place in the world. Constant reassessments. Not just what we deserve but what we need to be happy. Sometimes we feel we've failed because we don't have an en-suite bathroom even though we have many powerfully sustaining relationships and a widely envied hunger for adventure. Other days we feel that we should let it all go: leap off the property bus and see what happens. We'll never get back on, will we? Our house is our pension. We'll die on the streets surrounded by plastic bags stuffed full of property details muttering, 'Well, that budget will get you a fourth bedroom but forget about the underfloor heating…and is it near the railway line? Dirty.'

We define ourselves as 'in' or 'out' of the game by where we live and – worse, where we might live one day. We suffer from chronic house envy. The flung-together houses of people with not much money but ridiculously wonderful taste and/or incredible DIY skills. The design temples of those who manage never to buy rubbish and tat and generic 'middle class' markers. The vast monuments to money of the really, really, properly rich where the very air seems honeyed. The charming country retreats of those who relocated and now live a kind of chicken-populated dream life. Oh let's not forget the gyms and pools and playrooms. And just to be pedestrian, let us not forget loft-envy and extension-envy. Sometimes it can be as simple as front-door envy. Or even front path/step envy. We are not above going granular with our covetousness.

More. Boxes. To. Tick. More pressure. More porn. Wanting it doesn't make getting it any more likely. And getting it might not feel as good as property pornographers will lead us to believe. Just as porn isn't about real sex, property porn isn't about real life. But we are endlessly, bottomlessly compelled…

# Where Has All Our Money Gone?

Do you ever look back and think…all this money we've earned. What have we got to show for it? WHAT HAVE WE SPENT ALL OUR MONEY ON? Here's a broad-brushstrokes breakdown.

### 10 Per Cent On Minibreaks With Depressing Boyfriends That We Thought Might Be The One
Up and down the country staying in 'quirky' B&Bs. Trips to not-quite-Paris Continental cities like Valencia or Lille. We *paid* for this pain? In some ways we still are paying…

### 10 Per Cent On Therapy
It is worth it – isn't it? Because before that we were held together by bread, bits of self-help that we read in magazines, Spanx and the occasional yoga class/Xanax.

## 15 Per Cent On The Hunt For The Perfect Capsule Wardrobe

Is this the perfect white t-shirt? Is *this* the perfect white t-shirt? Is £70 too much for a white t-shirt? Will these black trousers work with everything forever? I hate them but will they? That white shirt, the one that gapes across the boobs, is that the one? God that coat is depressing. I have to have it.

## 5 Per Cent On Shoes That Don't Quite Fit

We thought maybe it didn't matter that we couldn't feel our toes. Or that eventually the blisters would heal and our feet would win.

## 35 Per Cent On Pointless Patching Of Leaks, Walls, Random Holes In Our Home

Because we can't afford to do the extension that needs doing. Maybe this nice vase will hide the damp? Maybe this witty poster will disguise the horror of the back of the house falling off. 'Rotten!' the man keeps saying while poking at the walls/roof/floor with a screwdriver. 'Rotten!' Oh, how we hate the man.

## 13 Per Cent On Taxis

Ubers, black cabs, dodgy minicabs, New York taxis, tuk-tuks. We have paid a heavy taxi tax.

## 645 Per Cent On Highlights

Also low-lights, and then fringes, and layers and then balayage and repairing shampoos, and root concealer, blow-dries. Extensions for the thinning. The thinning. The thinning…(that's how you type an echo…)

## 10.5 Per Cent On Phone Bills

Rewind to the day when you made all those phone calls. Now it's data, data, all that data. The awful French holiday where you accidentally spent 2k while roaming.

## 7 Per Cent On Athleisurewear

That has never seen the inside of a gym/yoga studio.

## 1 Per Cent On Dry-Cleaning

Because ironing.

**13 per cent on Food Fads**

We have fallen for EVERYTHING. Quick cookbooks, machines that turn frozen fruit into velvety yoghurty deliciousness, seeds all the seeds, especially the chia ones that are the price of black gold and spend an eternity in our front teeth and taste like frogspawn. Huge machines that will turn anything into a nutritious broth. Food boxes. Supplements. Sachets. We could go on but we need to go and sieve some boiled ginger water and raw honey, which, by the way, costs A MILLION POUNDS.

## Do You Have A Purse Full Of Hope?

I may be a millionaire. I may be a millionaire many, many times over. As I write, I have 14 unchecked lottery tickets in my purse. I buy two at a time: 'One lucky dip for today and one for tomorrow please,' I chirrup most Tuesdays and Fridays. That's 10 quid a week. Which is 40 quid a month. Which is £480 a year. Which is half my car insurance, a return flight to Ibiza high season, a whole winter outfit or most of an Isabel Marant Étoile coat. Apart from any of that, I should clearly be sending that money to refugees. Or Marie Curie. Because it's idiotic that I buy them and buy them and buy them…

But I get such dulcet pleasure from my faintly pulsating purse. No one else can feel the vibrations. No one else knows that I may be a millionaire many, many times over. And I find myself thinking, 'Should I even bother with Lotto? The jackpot is only £6 million, which clearly won't get me very far. Maybe I should focus on EuroMillions because that's a much more useful €72 million.' By the way, Brexit doesn't mean that we no longer qualify to be part of EuroMillions. I checked. Phew.

So you see what fun it is. The fantasy. The never quite knowing. The 'someone has to win'. When I'm paying for something or rummaging around for change I catch sight of my – potentially – pink ticket, and it makes me maybe infinitesimally nicer. Everyone needs a purse full of hope.

## If Your Bank Account Could Talk…

BA: You should know there has been fraudulent activity on your account.

Me: OMG.

BA: It's serious, I'm afraid.

Me: What????

BA: I've been monitoring erratic spending for some time.

Me: Christ, who is this bastard and how do we stop them?

BA: The thing is, there are almost no funds in your account, and that's what raised our suspicions.

Me: No need to rub it in, but go on.

BA: A designer dress was bought on Net-a-Porter.

Me: Hang on—

BA: And a handbag.

Me: Right. I do actually—

BA: And a belt that was definitely not worth £250.

Me: You say that, but—

BA: And then there was the flurry of eBay shopping at 4.30am last Thursday.

Me: Gosh, that sounds…I mean, who would…um?

BA: It was for a set of very overpriced glass bowls that will cost a fortune to be shipped from Milan.

Me: Wait, they were from Milan? Oh.

BA: Yes. This thief works internationally.

Me: Perhaps the thief was drunk after her sister's birthday party and ordered them by accident?

BA: Or perhaps they're just very reckless and stupid.

Me: Well, I don't know about—

BA: You would not BELIEVE how much this criminal is spending on Ocado.

Me: Errr…they might be a very busy criminal with no time to make it down to the supermarket.

BA: Who orders eight bottles of Comfort fabric conditioner in one go?

Me: Maybe it was on special offer for one weekend only and they thought it would be sensible to stock up?

BA: No one is that weird.

Me: …………………

BA: They seem to be supporting Deliveroo single-handedly.

Me: That sounds like an exaggeration, but—

BA: And Uber.

Me: Actually, they're pretty cheap, so—

BA: The point is, we're on to them.

Me: That's a…relief.

BA: So don't worry.

Me: (nervous laugh)

BA: They won't get away with it.

Me: (sounding shrill) So pleased.

# What Your Biscuit Says About You

1. McVities Rich Tea. Your house is entirely beige, like it has been dunked in tea. You don't wear animal print because you think it's showy and you have been going out with the same person since you were 15.
2. Viennese whirl. You are sexually experimental and VERY hard to please in bed. Staying in on a Friday night is social suicide for you. Terrible FOMO.
3. Jaffa Cake. You like to tell people you are gluten-intolerant and that you meditate every day, but it's all bullshit and deep down you crave pizza and acceptance.
4. Oreos. Exposed brick, stainless steel, Hermès bag, winters in Gstaad, summers in the Hamptons, friends with Gwyneth Paltrow since FOREVER, gold trousers that make you itch, heaving with diamond push presents, romantically involved with your tennis coach, weird dreams, love Disney.
5. Chocolate chip. You still sleep with your childhood toy and obsessively do Sudoku when you're stressed. You cry relentlessly during *X Factor* and want a pet rabbit. You still speak to your mother every day.
6. Jammie Dodger. Criminal record.
7. Ginger nut. You speak fluent French and are having an affair with a much older man (everyone has guessed by the way – it's the world's worst-kept secret).
8. Wagon Wheels. Chlamydia. It's hard to get rid of, isn't it?
9. Custard cream. You're always the most drunk person at the party and are excellent at swearing. You never forget a birthday and you can still do cartwheels.
10. Bourbons. Emotionally complicated, your dog is your best friend and, even though you know it's unhealthy and very much discouraged, so is your therapist. Being around the sheets in any bedding department is so calming. It is your safe space.

# 12 Really Annoying Ingredients

Store-cupboard staples, they say. Quick 'n' easy weekday suppers, they say. Oh.

### 1. Preserved Lemons

You know you're not going to use them. They're just sitting in a cupboard, looking like a menacing present from Hannibal Lecter. You're probably supposed to get all Ottolenghi on their arse and barbecue them with some sea bass or something, but we all know that's never going to happen.

## 2. Daikon

Why does it look so anaemic? Like someone bled it to save its life. What is it anyway? An ill radish?

## 3. Star Anise

Here's an idea. Why don't you add some star anise to your recipe so that everything now tastes overwhelmingly of aniseed and then forget to take it out so that you bite down on it and break your tooth/are sick because of the aniseed taste exploding in your mouth like a nuclear aniseed bomb of death?

## 4. Sumac

Want to make your fish taste really bitter? Sprinkle some sumac on it. If you can find it ANYWHERE, by the way. Honestly, shopping for the Holy Grail or Shergar would be easier.

## 5. White Pepper

OMG, just use black pepper and be done with it. Seriously.

## 6. Mullet

The bone situation here is off the chart. Each mouthful is so...whiskery. The bone-to-flesh ratio seems unreasonably in favour of bones and you have to fight to negotiate any fleshy bits from the overwhelming sense of skeleton currently clogging your mouth and entire eating experience.

## 7. Scotch Bonnets

Yeah, I can handle a bit of heat! I love it! Hit me with whatever you've got! Oh my Christ, someone hand me a fire extinguisher, MY HEAD IS BURNING. Relive the Great Fire of London in your own mouth by adding some Scotch bonnets to a recipe. Incinerate your taste buds and feel like someone flayed your tongue.

## 8. Capers

What this dish is missing is a sudden hit of vinegar, just when you were enjoying it. Slightly mushy, very unexpected. It's a BERRY, OK? It's, like, enhancing the texture and adding an element of surprise. The surprise being, what you thought you were going to enjoy you are now going to negotiate like someone tiptoeing through a field of landmines.

## 9. Red Rice

Cooking risotto with red rice is a mistake. What they don't tell you is that it will take you the rest of your life. You will have a dowager's hump and cataracts by the time it's ready. Prince George will be king, North West will have married Sir Carter and the sky will be full of electronic flying cars. Years from now, the rice will finally have absorbed enough water for you to not risk cracking your incisors on it. Just use Arborio and get your life back.

## 10. Chestnut Flour

What's it even doing in your cupboard? How did it get there and what does it want? It's been opened so you've obviously used it – but when? And why? Who were you when you bought it? What did that person want? What became of them?

## 11. Matcha

Now everything tastes of powdered nuts. Furthermore, you don't have more energy, nor do you have magical Inca powers or the secret of eternal youth – but you ARE less well off because that half-empty packet practically cost you a month's earnings.

## 12. Cream Of Tartar

So they got a sort of medieval Russian warrior and melted him down and turned him into a baking ingredient for CAKES? Why?

# Bog Standards

When we were growing up there was a vogue for cramming loos full of entertaining things. Witty things (for there were no smartphones). Loo books: piles and piles of them, each stickier and more yellowing than the last. And bottles of scent: each staler than the last. Small sculptural mounds of glued-together soaps: cracked, blackened, hairs of those who had gone before nestling in the crevices. Hand towels that weren't washed, just rehung.

We spend a lot of time in loos, don't we? Sometimes hiding/taking selfies/giving ourselves a talking to, sweatily struggling with zips, having a quick cry. And loos are not what they used to be. They are cleaner for a start. And emptier, praise be. So we know a thing or two about things that just shouldn't be there.

### Hand Cream

Every now and again you think gosh I must moisturise my hands because you know, GNARLED CLAWS. And so you see some in a loo somewhere and use it. And you are thrilled, thinking of course that hand wash and matching hand cream is just so civilised. Except you can't open the door. And, when you finally escape, you pick up a glass that immediately slides back onto the table and then you have to wipe your hands on your new skirt, which you don't realise until later is dry-clean only. And you remember why hand cream is evil.

## Cuddly Toys
Oh, hello Valentine's teddy cuddling a large, red heart. Oh, look, it's a vast, incredibly flammable penguin won at a fair that doubles as the dog's paramour. In fact, bits of it are definitely crusty. Also dolls…what are you looking at???

## A Lit Candle
Unattended, unattended, unattended. Don't you think we've got enough to worry about?

## Dried Flowers
Is it time to have a conversation about these? There is something morbid and horrific about your crunchy dead granny flowers sitting on the shelf of your bathroom, absorbing all the…action. They have clearly been there for years. Enough.

## Speakers
Yes, we know you've wired-up your whole house but, while Café del Mar is fine when chatting round the kitchen island, it is distinctly murdery when you're sitting alone on the throne. What are we meant to do? Dance?

## Thoughtlessly Placed Mirrors
Is there anything more awful than closing a door, sitting down and suddenly catching sight of the horror that is you on the loo. Gollum crossed with Jabba the Hutt. Quite hard to recover from this moment actually.

## No Phone Signal
WHAT IS EVEN THE POINT OF GOING?

## Framed Motivational Quotes
You know the ones that stare at you accusingly and make you feel crap about yourself: 'Collect moments not things' they say, and you think, 'Hold on I quite want those biker boots with the fake pearls so I can wade in fashion's shallows pretending to be a pirate.' Or, 'Fall seven times, stand up eight' and you think, 'Oh God but I am tired, so tired, all the women in me are tired.'

**Books**
Thumbed. Sweaty fingerprints. Unidentifiable stains. These are no longer OK. The ship has sailed.

# A Miditation On Fashion

As life unfurls itself around us and within us; as we ripen into who we are, we hope to throw off the weight of other peoples' expectations. Which leaves us dealing with the weight of our own expectations. And this is where fashion lives. Fashion. A big, clunky word. Self-conscious. Declamatory. Fashion: more about an industry than about a life. Let's deal with clothes and leave 'fashion' to the…professionals.

Clothes can make life better. The swish of a skirt. The woofle of cashmere. The flash of a brilliant boot. The dress that is a dream realised. Clothes are ours for the taking and, relatively recently, it has dawned on us in Western society that they are nobody else's business. Internet shopping has rendered the judgemental shop assistant the preserve of old movies because the delivery guy doesn't know what's in that box. The privacy of our own bedrooms is where we experiment. No face-saving, no panicking in the changing room. It works or it doesn't. There is very little we *should* not wear (except the waterfall cardigan, more of which later…)

Dress for the job you want, they say. Knock yourself out if that's your modus but, what about dressing for the day you want. For the rhythms and teeny, tiny crossroads of the hours ahead. Here is the only rule: one thing that you put on should give you joy. One thing should make you feel happy about what you are presenting, not necessarily to the world, but to those shop windows that snapshot us back at ourselves. Or the mirrors in lifts – someone once told me that the definition of elegance is not looking in lift mirrors and it seems like a valuable point of view, firstly, because they are so disheartening and secondly, because we all look so absurd pouting at them.

By the way, for clarity, when I say, 'one thing that gives you joy' I don't mean 'something fun'. There is a difference. This is not digging out a fun scarf or a fun brooch. This is about wearing something that makes you feel a bit relevant. Something that, if you were to catch sight of it on someone else, you might think, 'Oh, I like that… I'd wear that.' Because, too often we end up wearing a dispiriting fusion of what we can afford, what fits and what is kind of clean. And that leaves us no room to breathe.

Here's a word that's even sillier than 'fashion': 'edit'. Magazines and those 'tidy to be happy' books tell us to 'edit our wardrobe' by throwing away anything we haven't worn for a year. I think it would be better to throw away everything we don't like. You wouldn't have a fridge full of food you loathe. You wouldn't have a party full of people you hate. You'd have a horrible time. Don't have a horrible time. Don't write clothes off. Remind yourself that clothes can make the day a happier place and remember: it takes a lot of therapy to be this shallow.

## Step Away From The Waterfall Cardigan

There is no easy way to say this: ladies, step away from the waterfall cardigan. Whoever invented this bottomlessly cascading jumper situation was not thinking about allure, impact, energy or anything other than a hybrid of the two most sexless items of clothing around: the shawl and the cardi.

But somewhere along the line we became convinced that the waterfall cardigan was the common or garden cardigan's more elegant sister. 'Flowing lines' we told ourselves. 'Covers a multitude of sins' we may even have thought/said/hoped. It doesn't – it merely spotlights the fact that there are sins to hide. Waterfall cardigans tell the world that we are defeated.

In beige or pale grey we think they are classic. First of all, classic is rarely a compliment (and classic with a twist is always a horror story) and secondly, beige and pale grey can make cadavers of even the rosiest of us. The black waterfall tempts with its 'can't go wrong' message. Hmmm. If you think about it, they're properly witchy: great black swathes of knit. Navy is municipal, white is criminal and as for cheerful bright colours? Book your sunset cruise now.

The waterfall cardigan is the new elasticated waist in a world where everything is stretchy. Except it is more insidious than the elasticated waist because it pretends to be glamorous.

But we can't be critical without being constructive so, as a consolation prize we give you…the A-line jumper. Possibly in Breton. Perhaps with a flared sleeve. Varying in length from waist down to mid-thigh depending on your proportions. Great with a flashy pencil skirt, good with a jean, perfect with the pandemic of athleisurewear. It's a waterfall that hasn't completely lost touch.

## Funderwear Vs. Thunderwear

At some point in life, you make a choice between funderwear and thunderwear. Knickers to be seen in or knickers to be yourself in. If you are wearing knickers to potentially please someone else then the wearing of those knickers is giving your power away. If you want to sexually politicise your pants. Which, on second thoughts, we don't. Too worthy. But the thing about funderwear is, it's not that much fun. In the end. *picks string out of crack*

There is no shame in big pants. Really there isn't. Particularly when it's autumn and we are feeling chilly and insecure. Big pants are a cuddle. True, there is something faintly disheartening about a multipack of full briefs, but what about those vast cotton numbers that they sell in every single street market (from Puglia to Lincolnshire) for a single pound/euro? Love those.

Big pants not only make you feel held, they often give you the last laugh, being so enormous that they read as largely seam-free, riding – as they do – so high on the tum and so low on the bottom. No lumps and bumps.

And there is a sod's law aspect to the larger knicker. Rather like a hairy leg or a big, bouncing bush: somehow you're more likely to have spontaneous sex when you are not groomed or uniformed for it. Freedom. That's what big pants give you. Freedom to have a big dinner. Freedom to flirt without (or even with) consequence. Freedom not to constantly adjust the cheese wires digging into your sides. Oh, and for the record, a substantial boy short counts as a big pant. So unflattering. So easy. So the way forward. Leave the floss-smalls in the drawer. And unleash hell.

## Because You Can Never Have Enough Storage

Coins. Phones. Tissues. Credit cards. Keys. These are small things. They are also things you need to access quick smart. Handbags? Well I don't know about you, but mine contain a floating and ever-evolving mass of gently disintegrating matter. Eyeliners without lids. Headphones tangled into intriguingly unassailable masses. Budless cotton buds. Empty ibuprofen packets, forever separated from their cargo. Flurries of receipts. A single earring. A chocolate wrapper I have tried to hide from myself. It's a jungle in there.

And so I keep my immediate necessities in my bra. Yes, my boobs are large. Yes, my bras are large, which means that the surface area and potential for storage space is generous. Not rucksack generous. But certainly micro-clutch-bag generous.

It started when I used to go clubbing. Money, fags, whatever, tucked into my bra. Yes, it probably compromised my silhouette but I was – and generally am – more concerned with convenience than perfection. Perfection is for other people.

Change for parking meters always sits in my bra. And, when I fling it off at the end of the day, the leftover pound coins clatter to the floor leaving me with the pleasing thought that, 'Oh, my breasts make money.' I light candles or my daily cigarette and tuck the lighter into my bra so that I don't lose it. The result? A bathroom cabinet stuffed with Clippers but none whatsoever down in the kitchen.

I like dresses. They tend to have no pockets. I like jeans but I don't like digging in tight ones for coins and iPhones have grown too big for jean pockets. And so my bra is my go to storage space. Raise your hand if you have enough storage in your life. See?

# The Chair

Let's talk about The Chair. The Chair in your bedroom. The draping, dumping chair where clothes sit in limbo: too dirty for the cupboard, too clean for the laundry.

But, hang on a second, if they are too clean for the laundry, if they have another wear in them before they need to be dealt with, then why can they not slot virtuously back onto a shelf or into a drawer? I mean, are we worried that they may *infect* the imagined sterility of the wardrobe? Do we feel that they are too sullied by life to consort with the irreproachable purity of the put-away items? We do. It's mad but we do.

Chair occupants have no rights. They are refugees from the cupboard who, as yet, have not won their pass to redemption. They disgust us a little. They trouble us a lot.

Our disgust is reflected back at us every time we catch sight of The Chair whose very existence seems to mirror the chaos in our heads.

Jeans. There are always jeans. Jeans too grubby to associate with the righteous jeans in the land of Put Away. Chair jeans are, firstly, a visual prompt towards the nagging realisation that there are some thinner jeans in the cupboard. There is probably a pair in there worn only once – possibly after a vicious bout of norovirus or heartbreak. They were a triumph on that one day and have been a cruel talisman of failure ever since. The jeans on The Chair are also a nose-wrinkling reminder that we wash jeans perhaps ten times less than any other everyday thing that we own. Partly because the dirt doesn't register until things have got properly chronic and partly because post-wash jeans are just rubbish. If cleanliness is next to godliness then jeans remind us that we are heathens, heretics, the fallen. Jeans represent the human condition and so The Chair is their natural home. They deserve no better.

Jumpers get a little less loveable every time they are laundered. Even when hand-washed with baby shampoo and dried flat they lose a little of their lustre. And so, when we are at a loose end and confronted with The Chair, we might pick up a dark-coloured jumper and pick away at a stain as though it were a scab. We tell ourselves that The Chair will 'air' them. It won't.

Similarly, we are airing the gym kit that we didn't *really* get sweaty in. We only wore it for 45 minutes so it would be an ECO-DISASTER to wash it now. It would be actually immoral. And so it lies there – limp and accusatory – until we get one more workout session out of it. But it's been a week now, so not only are we filthy, we are lazy and bad.

Oh hello, dry-clean-only pile. How do we hate you? Let's count the ways. First of all, who can afford dry-cleaning? Second of all, who is organised enough to take it to the dry-cleaners and also pick it up? Thirdly, are dry-cleaners even trustworthy? Will they lose it? Will they turn it a funny colour? Maybe we should risk it and put it on a cold wash? Soon we shall decide. Until then we'll leave it on the chair as a reminder.

It's only been six months.

Probably best we don't talk about the devil's repair mound. The frock with the rip in the side seam from…not sure. We were drunk. The cashmere that needs darning. First of all, what is darning? Second of all, the bastard moths are bound to get it again just as they are gnawing through everything in the house. Zara are selling those sweaters with ready-made 'derelict' holes in them. We tried one recently and it made us look both destitute and unhinged. Anyway, no need to pay for holey, wrecked jumpers when here they sit. On. The. Chair.

The Chair feels like a sneering manifestation of our failures. It's the monkey on our back, the albatross around our neck, the sparrow of disappointment twittering in our ears. Some days. Other days it's just the chair in the corner, the one that shows us that perfection is for other people. The one that gives us a little wriggle room between the laundry and the cupboard.

## Time To Say Goodbye…

…to the things in your wardrobe that are probably past their sell by date. They are, aren't they? You know they are. Time to woman up.

### 1. Designer Sale Shoes
If sales weren't such competitive environments, you might not find yourself the proud owner of three pairs of Jimmy Choos, all of which cost £80, two of which are two sizes too small. Sales are the human equivalent of throwing raw meat to piranhas. You've never worn them. You physically can't wear them. You don't even like them that much.

### 2. The Plaid Shirt
You thought it made you look adorable, possibly even rather sexy like Daisy Duke. Actually, it just makes you look a bit violent. Like one of the toothless hillbillies in *Deliverance* coupled with the undeniable masculinity of Burt Reynolds.

### 3. Too Sexy Underwear
Remember that moment of strange otherness, where you got a bit drunk and ordered yourself some *slightly* sexy underwear online. And when it arrived, you tried to talk yourself out of the knowledge that it gave you double-boob and a brutal and unflattering wedgie? You've never worn it – but there it sits, staring at you in all your failure.

### 4. An Ex-Boyfriend's T-Shirt
The one that's been washed so many times it is baby soft and looks vintage. The one

you slept in while he was away. The one you were wearing when he cried because his PowerPoint crashed or the time he couldn't get it up or the time he told that creepy story about how good-looking his sister was and you started to go off him.

### 5. The Whore Dress
That dress so short you give the world a LOOK AT ME view of your vagina. Or the backless dress that was, to be honest, slightly frontless too so no chance of a bra.

### 6. Terrible Handbags
The fake Fendi baguette with the lollipop in the pocket denoting the fact that you haven't used it since you last went clubbing and that was during Queen Victoria's reign. The Dior saddlebag in pink that made you look like a drunk estate agent.

### 7. The Military Overcoat With Too Many Flaps And Buttons
Sorry, are you auditioning for Janet Jackson's *Rhythm Nation* ensemble? Did you try to defend enemy lines and fight back Napoleon's armies during the Battle of Borodino? Are you Kenneth Branagh in *Dunkirk*? Were you one of the 'Revolutionary Nuns' tasked with the private protection of Colonel Gaddafi?

### 8. The Cheap High Street Gypsy Top
OK, you're not 12 and you're not a gypsy. Time to come to terms with both of those things. Perhaps.

### 9. Stupidly High Heels
The heels so high they make you walk like you're recovering from a double hip replacement.

### 10. The Jumper You Shouldn't Keep Washing
That cashmere one you couldn't be arsed to get dry-cleaned and washed on cold but still it emerged as a crop top.

## Chapter 5

# WHAT'S NORMAL ANYWAY?

YOU MAY OR MAY NOT HAVE NOTICED that, generally, there are no children in this book. They have been lovingly removed. There are many awesome places and ventures and conversations that revolve around motherhood, and this is not one of them. There are, broadly, two reasons for this. First, this book is about identity. It is about recognising each other as stand-alone creatures with vast tracts of emotional common ground. Not just as mothers or sisters or employees or daughters.

The second reason that this is – largely – a child-free zone, is because of pain. And grief. And misunderstanding. And hell, actually. In researching the Midult mindset, in getting to know our people and learning what mattered to them – what made them laugh and cry and rage and panic, we uncovered a disconnect between women in conventional relationships who have children, and women who are 40 and beyond without conventional relationships or children. We sat there again and again and watched a kind of hideous tennis match between the two. 'Oh lucky you, think of all the shoes you can buy and the holidays you can take,' ventured one well-meaning mother of two with a head tilt (the universal language of pity) to a 41-year-old single woman who was able to do nothing other than shoot a watery smile across the table. 'They're overrated,' said another married-at-30-naturally-pregnant-at-32 type, 'I'd trade them in for a lie-in.' Who knew there was such a monumental and painful lack of communication between those drunk on the cult of parenthood and those sitting outside?

I have a child. I had a child by myself. Not in the 'we all die alone' sense but in the 'I made this happen' sense. I slowly became convinced that, even though I was single, I was capable of making my life more the way I wanted it to be. Hell, the way I needed it to be.

Let me break down for you how it can feel to be hitting 40 without a baby when a baby is all you've ever wanted. People talk about biological imperative striking as menopause hoves into view but I had wanted a baby for years. More than anything. More than a perfect man or a brilliant career. 'What are you really?' Some career life coach type asked me when I was about 36. 'A mother.'

But the vicissitudes of life did not align with my desire. And, despite what hitherto accepted wisdom might have you believe, it was not because I was too picky or because I put my career first. In my experience it never, ever, is. It is far more likely to be sheer bloody, bloody-minded, bad bloody luck.

I was 38 and I had never been married and I had no children. How could I have no children? How could I look that in the face? And apart from the grief and the panic and the weariness, I was overwhelmed by silent shame. By broken expectations. By terror that the desperation I felt in my heart was visible. Each birthday party felt like a wake. Each baby shower like bathing in acid. And during our Midult meetings some of the women without children started to talk about the shame. And some of the women with children started to listen.

We talked about how we had developed a kind of internal monologue of despair. All we could see, walking down the street, driving in the car, were babies and bumps. And we hated these blooming women. We silently called them names. We navigated department stores to cunningly swerve baby departments, we turned off nappy adverts on the telly, we cried when we had to go and visit fresh babies held, in grotty hospital beds, by radiantly proud mothers. We admitted that looking at a childless future felt like looking at death. And I felt like a facilitator of these discussions because, despite having a child, the pain was still real to me; accessible. I hadn't forgotten.

I was single when I conceived one lovely summer's evening in a very nice doctor's office. I was single when I gave birth. But I feel false when I declare myself to be a single mother. I feel that I am doing me and my lot a disservice. I am a single person but a solo mother. Single somehow suggests a mistake, or a break-up with that whiff of romantic tragedy. That didn't happen. I just decided to proceed. Solo. A solo voyage. We are solo mothers. And, suddenly, we are everywhere. There are seven solo mothers in my address book and two more going solo almost as we speak with many, many more considering it. This is the crest of the wave. We are about to be everywhere. Not lesbian couples. Not gay men using surrogates. Just women – sexuality put entirely aside for now – choosing to override romantic circumstances in favour of parenthood. For now, I stress. This isn't a spinsters-with-kids club.

By the way it's terrifying (even though my child has a wonderful father – we made an arrangement). But you learn – and any woman who's had a child by herself, or had eight cycles of IVF, or used an egg donor, or started a new business, or left a shitty partner, or explored relatively uncharted territory in myriad ways, will know this: you are only as brave as what you want. Desire and intent get results.

My first step towards solo motherhood, although I didn't know it at the time, came after the break-up of a major relationship. I was 36 and we were going to be together forever. That decision had been made. And then suddenly, in a horribly pedestrian way, it was unmade. It was as though we'd lost our keys…except is was the love that we had lost. 'But, hang on! I had it a minute ago. Where did I put it?' Gone. And, amid physically and mentally melting from shock, I found myself at the women's clinic having the fertility test package. Wall-to-wall couples lining walls lined with poster-sized pictures of babies. Jesus. An internal scan and two blood tests later I discovered that I had Optimum Fertility. Of course, not all probability can be captured biochemically, but this gave me an overview. Knowledge means choices. Knowledge helps counter potential regret. Knowledge, as ever, is power.

Two years later, when I revisited these results with true focus, it started to dawn that fertility is like a card game: you have no idea what move to make until you understand what has just happened and process that information. Everything raises as many questions as it answers. I call it the Eggscalator. And, when you hop on the Eggscalator, you have no idea where it will take you. Could be that you get spooked, hop off and consider it dealt with. Or maybe it will lead you to bulldoze through all your firmly held deal-breakers – egg donation, adoption, surrogacy, endless drugs, huge financial burden and massive emotional pressure. Just as flirtations can become obsessions, so an open-hearted glance in fertility's general direction can set you on a course to God knows where. And, if you are sitting on the loo, staring at a pregnancy test after multiple rounds of treatment, willing it to be positive, then God will almost always come into it. But remember that couples who get drunk and shag on the sofa and then go 'Oops!' do not know about the Eggscalator. It is for the special people. And it can take you to the heart of who you are and what you want.

We need to claim the phrase 'Solo Mother'. It needs to belong to us because we have made a big, bold, brave, beautiful choice. It may not be 'The Dream'. It is a different dream. These babies are the opposite of accidents. They didn't happen to us. If anything, we happened to them.

## Thinking Of Having A Baby By Yourself?

Here are some things you should know:

1. Married women will tell you that all men are useless and that it's no harder to do it by yourself. They are wrong.
2. Married women will tell you that they envy your ability to focus on your baby because you don't have a husband to entertain/shag/keep. They are right.
3. Single pregnancy is by far the weirdest thing about single motherhood.
4. If you have even the slightest scrap of spare cash when you are pregnant, buy yourself a present. You are about to really deserve a present but you will remain bottom of your own list for some time.
5. You will not be ready to meet somebody 'as soon as you've got your figure back'. You really won't care for a couple of years.
6. Having a baby is intensely romantic and – seeing as there is no partner to feel

jealous or threatened – inhale that mutual fascination.

7.  The money side of things is far and away the most stressful part. You have to be incredibly grown-up about dealing with this.

8.  There isn't a stigma.

9.  You will astound yourself with your disgustingness. But you'll prefer time with your baby to any grooming.

10. Careful with the tiredness. Even if you've got guts when it comes to sleep deprivation, remember it's cumulative. If you start to feel mad, rope some bodies in. You do have to ask.

11. Surprising people leave your life and others enter it in meaningful ways. Go floppy and let them come and go.

12. Once you emerge from the baby bubble (18 months or so) you will come face-to-face with unprecedented and unanticipated ambition. Your own.

## 'Why Did She Never Marry?'

I am 42 and a spinster. I am not married and I have never been married. Might I get married? I suppose it's possible. I feel no wild yearnings but nice to think that the universe has left that particular door open. Like those ladies you read about who marry the man they thought they had lost in the war at 91.

But there is a deeply dispiriting phrase that I hear when people talk about women from their late thirties onwards and it is this: 'Did she never marry?' My mother did it the other day and added a sparkling addendum: 'Did she never marry? What's *wrong* with her?'

I didn't grow up dreaming of a spring wedding and sketching a dress but that doesn't mean I haven't thought about what a wedding – or a marriage – might be like. I still wonder. And though I don't long for the pealing of church bells and the sparkling of a diamond ring (are engagement rings a bit silly?), I do allow my mind to drift now and again. Is that tragic? Am I, in my early forties, basically dead when it comes to matrimony? Is it undignified to consider it? If I ever did get married would I have to wear a skirt suit?

We are told and told and told that women over the age of 35 are more likely to be struck by lightning than to get married. OK. But can't I please be unmarried rather than unmarry-able? To humour me if nothing else? Condemning the late bloomers to life alone seems a little ungenerous. Because by this time in life we have learnt that anything can happen. And sometimes it does.

# 10 Things Not To Say To A Woman With No Children

1. You'd better get a move on.
2. Lucky you – your bits are intact!
3. You've never known love until you're a mother.
4. I don't know about all that fertility treatment – it probably causes cancer. They really don't know.
5. I just think it's a bit selfish to be an older mother. It's not natural, you know?
6. I'd give them both up for one good night's sleep.
7. I mean that's what we are here for…oh sorry…
8. When's it due?
9. Did you never WANT kids?
10. It's not all it's cracked up to be.

## 'You've Got Kids, Right?'

The other day I was having my hair cut and a lady at the nail bar was wanging on about her new puppy. 'Up all hours,' she was saying. 'So tired. No rest.' And then she turned to me: 'You've got kids, right?' Why? Because I'm in my forties and relatable looking? A bit like her, like you? Every woman? Nothing ostensibly wrong? Nothing ostensibly special? Just, y'know, living?

That assumption is so stupid and so hurtful. Firstly, because fewer and fewer of us are having kids. Secondly, because – for all the child-free empowerment movement, which I wholeheartedly and passionately support – I have, in my life, met possibly two women who didn't have children as an active choice. Failed IVF? Yup. Failed marriage? Yup. Failed to find a man in time? Mostly. And not because of career focus or selfishness or anything other than mis-timing, misfortune and mistakes. And generally – although there are exceptions – it has been a personal tragedy that has required committed grieving.

So do not assume. Do not do it. Every time you do, it is a stab to the heart of a woman who can't see for prams and nappy adverts and fecund bumps. The only thing that fills a baby-shaped hole is a baby, and if that's not possible then things get complicated. And dark. More complicated than the mother-club can imagine. Do not assume and do not tilt your head and look sympathetic. It is not your business. Do not bring it into the hairdresser. The pain does not belong there…That is where we go to escape.

## How To Horrify Your Teenage Stepchildren

Are you on holiday in a blended-family kind of way? Oh, LUCKY YOU! That's relaxing. You must be happy. A lovely, trouble-free break from all things stressful. Anyway, here are ten things you should never say to your teenage stepchildren. Unless you want to really mess with their heads...

1. Can I borrow a pair of knickers?
2. Your mother sounds absolutely insane.
3. If I don't get laid tonight I am going to go mad.
4. What are you even doing here?
5. You've put on weight.
6. That's my cheese.
7. You are in the spare room (every other weekend for the rest of your childhood).
8. I never had spots.
9. At some point you might want to do something about that nose.
10. I've brought a tutor. SURPRISE!

## 'How's Your Marriage?'

How was your first date? Did you kiss? Has he texted? Oh my God, first minibreak? Aargh – better get a Brazilian and stock the fridge with cranberry juice. How is the sex? How much? How many times? How experimental? No!!!!!!!! Really???????? That's got to sting. And he doesn't annoy you? Wow, he's that supportive? That funny? Amazing...

And so on and so forth...chat, chat, chat. Every detail. What position? What restaurant? What shared values? What family politics? How's it going? Do you think you'll move in? Do you think you'll get married? YOU'RE GETTING MARRIED!!!!!

And then. Silence. No one asks those questions. Those very friends with whom you shared eye-watering details just abandon you to your fate. Do they feel it would be impertinent to ask if you and your husband still have rude sex? Still have any sex? And, sex aside, no one wants to know if you are still talking, laughing, managing? The best you get is 'What about a baby?', which as discussed above is a damn stupid question these days.

So, how's your marriage? Are you OK? Are you feeling yourself within it and is there anything we can do to help? Come on Midults. Talk to each other. Even an 'I sense all might not be brilliant so do talk to me if that would help and I'll happily forget everything you tell me immediately' would be an excellent start. Because, married or single, life doesn't move in a straight line. It's not disloyal to talk and it's not intrusive to ask. Talk is not always gossip. Talk is not always cheap. Sometimes it's priceless.

## To All The Women Out There Who Leave

Dear women who leave,

We are the same – you and I. We are the 'had enoughs', the 'won't take it anymores', the 'ones who decided'. The end happened on our watch. We snapped.

And history will judge us for it. It is and will remain the first fact people share in discussion about us. No matter how much time passes. They will describe our former partners and husbands as 'lovely, so nice' – because the left are always lovely, you see. Regardless of what went on, they are the saints, the victims, the baffled. But we never wanted to be any of those things anyway.

People struggle to accept our decision, call our homes 'broken' and become suspicious of us. There is something deeply unnerving about women who take the plunge, shed an old life and plough on to a new – untested – version of happiness. People don't like it. They are sceptical at best, downright appalled at worst. We are the villains. We are the baddies. Ruthless, selfish, devil women. Emma Thompson will never play us in the big screen story of our lives.

Because there is still a stigma around our kind. I bumped into someone recently, a couple of years after she'd left. She'd endured decades of let's say 'nonsense' – all kinds – and stayed until she could bear it no longer. By the end of our conversation we were both in tears. Parting, she said, 'Thank you for talking to me, so many people don't anymore.'

The truth is some friends don't want this version of us. We're dangerous now. Or perhaps they just don't want to talk about the ins and outs. Socially, we are harder to compartmentalise after we leave.

We'll never go back. You can't persuade us or haunt us with 'you'll never find anyone else who'll take you on/love you like that'. We've got plans for something better. The truth about life with the person we left? Well, that isn't your business, but it did not work. Yes, this means we're alone. Yes, at times we panic. But this is life on our own terms.

So OK, we are the baddies. And yes, we will be recorded as the mad, bad women. But we'll take it on the chin and shake off the shame. So Emma Thompson will never, ever play us. But Julia Roberts might.

# 10 Things You Still Lie To Your Mother About

1. The fact you haven't been to the dentist for three years.
2. That you shagged your cousin when you were 17, on that family holiday in France.
3. That you showed up really drunk to babysit number 34's children when you were 15 and then fell asleep on the sofa.
4. Excel? Of course you know how to use it. Just like you can speak Spanish.
5. Obviously you fed her cat twice a day while she was away.
6. 'Sure you can meet him.'
7. That you don't smoke.
8. That you will look after her (psychotic) cat when she dies.
9. That you are putting a little bit aside for that rainy day.
10. That you know exactly where Granny's pearl earrings are.

## Welcome to Midulthood

# SECRET MIDULT BEHAVIOUR

1. Improv edgy dance moves in front of the mirror – dabbing anyone? The running man? Yup, still got it.
2. Hiding when the doorbell rings.
3. Eating things like peanut butter on celery and hot chocolate mix straight from the tub while standing in the kitchen.
4. Imagining heroic scenarios where you are a secret agent or being interviewed by Kirsty Wark on *Newsnight*: 'Well, I am glad you asked that, Kirsty...'
5. Talking to inanimate objects: shouting at the TV, telling the toaster it's a cunt (because it IS).
6. Taking selfies you never intend to share that are basically just checking out how weird your face is or what it does when you lie down. Also topless selfies. Just to see...
7. Hiding money. Could be a secret account. Could be under the bed.
8. Bad body stuff like picking feet, squeezing spots, plucking hairs. All while talking...for example to the chin hair: 'Out you come, you little fucker.'
9. Suddenly standing up with true purpose as though on a mission to call a cab and go to Bali and never come back, but really just going to get more chocolate and sitting back down on the sofa.
10. Trying on old, really sexy underwear. The stuff from another life.
11. Talking to yourself in the third person. Using surnames: 'Pull yourself together, Rivkin.' 'Come ON, McMeekan.'

## Chapter 6

# NOBODY PUTS MIDULTS IN THE CORNER

THIS IS NOT A BIG RANT about women in the workplace, about all the attempts to get more 'birds on boards', about the fact that the tensile pressure of office doors were tested by large men and are usually really heavy for our lady arms. That is one micro-reason why, in myriad ways, we feel that we don't always belong in the world, let alone in the workplace. There are fewer female CEOs than there are CEOs named John. But this is not a rant about women in the workplace.

Despite all the conversations and the campaigns and the awareness and the high-profile women throwing themselves under the work horse, there is no level playing field yet. And I have to confess I am not sure I want to play on it at all anymore. I was brought up to see work as a series of goals, each goal an ending in itself. It's a very straight-line way of thinking. And life does not tend to move in a straight line.

I was goal-greedy. I went to a high-powered girls school, full of high-powered girls, and nearly everyone became a lawyer or a stay-at-home mother. I went to a high-powered university and I went into magazines and then newspapers. I've slowly climbed the ladder of my profession. Or have I? Have I not just ping-ponged from job to job without a plan? The only time I actually made a plan – to ask for a pay rise – it was denied. I had a biggish job, definitely a career highlight, one that I was incredibly proud of, one that I loved. I shined the spotlight on young talent. I made them stars. I was at my desk, bright-eyed every morning at 7am. No one ever saw me in a bad mood. And yet as the climate changed and people left and weren't replaced, and it became tougher and tougher, and more and more was asked of me, the pressure began to hurt, my personality began to privately malfunction. So I thought I would ask for a pay rise: let's put a price on this pain. This is straight-line thinking, right?

Any of you who has ever woman-ed up and asked for more money, practised in the mirror and tried to override their natural apology system, will know how long this decision took. So I asked, and I was told no. That the ones to be given pay rises were younger; they were 'the stars' said the (male) management. So I resigned. 'You cannot see my star,' I thought. And then they said, 'Oh no, stay, we'll give you the money.' But it was too late. Now I wanted to be a star in my own damn sky.

I wanted more. I was ambitious for myself and for my tribe. And let's face it, ambition is a hard word for women, so nuanced, so double-edged. We've all worked for women who are arseholes and not just because they were pretending to assimilate. But after years of wrestling in the workplace, wrapped in a label that didn't fit, I realised that I was ambitious for work where I could be a woman without pretending to be a ball-breaker or a floosie. Where other women aren't threats but rather strings to your bow. You can say confidently, 'this is where I end but it is where another woman begins'. Where no one sits above like Zeus, directing his mini-universe with fire balls of fear and the odd comment on my tits.

So hey, we are in new territory. These are new foundations we women are building, baby brick by baby brick. Everywhere you look there are female-led micro-economies blossoming – by women, for women.

And we've been paying attention. We've been watching, we've seen your Lehman Brothers and your Northern Rocks and your 'too big to fail'. We've sat in your boardrooms (just barely), on your chairs (ugly), we've tried the networking and the 'lunch is for wimps'. And maybe we don't want what he's having.

It's a quiet rebellion. Women don't start wars with guns. But we are an army of women who have looked – really looked – and said, 'No thanks – I'll do it this way.' But as I said, this is not a rant about women in the workplace. This is about…well…let's see.

## 10 Things You Only Know If Your First Office Job Was In The Nineties

1. The thrill of sending an email to the person sitting next to you just to say 'Hi'.
2. You could only answer emails at your desk in the office.
3. It was the last decade of weekday lunchtime drinking. Only one. Bottle.
4. You could contentedly play computer solitaire for at least an hour a day.
5. Lunch was terrible soup or a terrible sandwich. Later on in the decade it was terrible sushi.
6. SO MUCH POST. Opening letters was fun.
7. People thought you were a bit weird if you went to the gym.
8. Until 1998 you had to look things up in a paper book or ask someone who knew stuff. You might do this by phoning them up and actually speaking to them. Once upon a time this was not weird or scary.
9. Getting a fax was always a low-level trip. A bit like getting flowers. Except not.
10. The invention of posh coffee. Lattes! So sophisticated! So expensive! So many calories!

# The End Of Work/Life Balance

'How's your work/life balance?' they ask.

'Really great,' replies no one ever.

Work/life balance is in itself a self-punishing phrase conjuring up, as it does, that image of scales, of justice. And seeing as things take constant readjustment, constant tweaking, you are set up for guaranteed failure. Because balancing generally involves falling the fuck over, and shifting from foot to foot, rhythm to rhythm, life to life. At work, too often we find that we are putting one hat on, replacing it with a mask, covering that with a cloak and then pretending to have a limp while doing an impression of a parrot. Then getting home, ripping out our actual or metaphorical shoulder pads and somehow reverting to our cosy selves.

What if we were to let go of this strange notion of balance? In fact, what if we were to actively reject it. In favour of something like…work/life integration. A notion that we could be ourselves at all times – with our boundaries and our fears and our motivations – and stop trying to dance to all the different tunes that the great DJ in the universe chucks into our soundtracks.

Work/life balance was for a time of landlines and faxes, presenteeism and office hours. Now that some of those shackles have loosened, others have tightened. Those times – particularly for women – were about 'the juggle'. Which in itself threatens constantly dropped balls. Integration is inclusive; gathering the good and the necessary towards you and growing through it all. Rather than standing, shield in hand, ever-terrified of tumbling and stumbling and failing. Integrate. Unleash the power and potential of all the colours in your rainbow. Sure, you might trip, But who's looking?

# All The Bosses We've Had

### The Thief

Ruthlessly appropriates your ideas (there's no I in team, right?) and you start finding yourself writing their emails and then their thank you letters; choosing their lunch and then their clothes. And suddenly you are lending out your funniest most brilliant, warm-hearted self to this soul-sucking dementor. Hold on, is it weird that you are picking up their dry-cleaning and giving up your Saturday to help them move house and it's been a while since you were a PA. And then you realise that your boss is a thief and is nicking your life.

### The Intriguer

Drops delicious titbits about the company fortunes. Gossips about the directors and other staff. But you, you are in the inner sanctum. You are called into the meeting room five minutes before anyone else and 'Oh just stay behind a second' so you can laugh at everyone else. For the first two years you feel safe, privileged, you're slightly aglow, then all of a sudden you realise that you would pay not to have to sit in a room with this person ever again. And that everyone hates you.

### The Insane One

Ricocheting like a pinball from one decision to another – there is no anticipating this lunatic so you end up doing endless damage limitation – and you have to do everything twice. You are shouted at and humiliated and you are pushed to breaking point almost every single day. You get really good at your job. And the boss's job. Grrr.

### The Powerhouse

For years you slept at your desk, chained to your computer, your entire mission to fuel the powerhouse. The powerhouse is growing the company, the powerhouse is a force of nature. The powerhouse is an expert at managing up. You really admire the powerhouse but you are not sure you like them. You adopt some of their mannerisms and hate yourself for it. Your mother worries.

### The Crush

They are gorgeous. So nice and funny and clever, and you have never actually worked for someone you both liked and admired. You start off shy and get a little more confident each day and you are, hold on, blossoming. You will never hear a word said against this boss for the rest of your life. You feel about them the way posh men feel about their nanny.

### The Faddish One

If you're not feng shui-ing the office, you're doing goat yoga and positive visualisation. You – and the whole department – develop a gothic horror of away days as you end up either doing a tough mudder or being rebirthed. This boss is the most competitive of the lot.

## Stressed? You've Got Nothing On Hand Sanitiser Woman

How stressed are you at work? We only ask because one woman we heard about – Angie Payden, a banker in Wisconsin – became so panicked with her job at a bank that she started swigging hand sanitiser. Hand sanitiser. Pause. Obviously you are not that stressed. But...

> One morning, before meeting with a customer, in which I knew I was going to have to sell unneeded services, I had a severe panic attack. I went to the bathroom and took a drink of some hand sanitiser. This immediately reduced my anxiety. From that point, I began drinking the hand sanitiser all over the bank. In late November 2012, I was completely addicted to hand sanitiser and drinking at least a bottle a day during my workday.

For your information and for context, a bottle of hand sanitiser has about five shots of alcohol in it. Good to know. So here are some other solutions to office stress before you head for the HypaClean:

1. Find a tribe. According to research, the single biggest key to surviving the office jungle is a group of like-minded individuals who will support you and drink actual shots with you if necessary. The key is connection.
2. Learn to say no. No means no. As in, 'No, I'm not going to do that.' Practise in front of the mirror. While you are there, practise asking for a pay rise.
3. Go on holiday. No one will thank you for staying in the office for all the hours/days/months, just as they won't thank you for drinking all the hand sanitiser.
4. Take off your shoes. Copy the Finnish gaming company Supercell, which asks its employees to remove their shoes before coming into the office. Apparently it's relaxing and productive. It turns out that at Supercell each employee is worth at least $5 million. *removes shoes immediately*
5. Browse the net for cute animal pictures.

## Warning: Ambitious Content

Ambition is not a dirty word, they told us. We needed to feel free to access our ambition. 'I am ambitious,' we cried. But what if ambition is heavy and hard and oppressive? What if we have become so wedded to the idea of our own ambition that we can hardly breathe? What if – without taking a gap year or moving to the arse-end of nowhere – we want to take a break from the very idea of ambition? And, by the way, 'She's very ambitious' is never used by one woman to compliment another. So, while we are supposed to be ambitious, we use it as a stick to beat each other with. If we ourselves are ambitious then we can be assured that it is tempered with compassion and wisdom. But if we label another woman as ambitious, we are being reductive. It is a term only ever used to denote fake admiration with a hint of 'Watch out…Ambitious is about'.

I'd like to release myself from ambition. It has to be OK to admit that ambition could mean being able to work a little less and financially relax a lot more. An expansion of self rather than a clamber upwards. Otherwise we're attaching a label to our motivations that feels punishing. That feels as though ambition is a step to activate superiority rather than personal joy. And feeling superior and special is one sure-fire way to feel isolated and anxious. Now that traditional corporate structure has relaxed to the point of becoming almost unrecognisable, have women connected with their motivation and their drive only to find themselves locked in an outdated ambition box where it loses its magic? I no longer know if I am ambitious. But I do feel hungry for life. Is that the same thing?

## Conversations You Have With Yourself In A Meeting

Me:        Please God let no one ask me anything.

Also me:  If I reach for that croissant within the first five minutes of this meeting starting, will I look greedy?

Me:        If anyone asks me anything, I'm going to set the fire alarm off.

Also me:  Wait, is that a pain au chocolat?

Me:        God, is that thing they're talking about my responsibility?

Also me:  FFS, will someone just take a croissant so I can?

Me:        Who is Peter in accounts anyway???

Also me:  I've had my soul hijacked by a French pastry.

Me:        Why have I already got 25 new emails? I've only been in here for 12 seconds.

Also me:  No, don't go for the chocolate one, go for the plain one, it looks more restrained.

Me:        Why am I being copied in on things I have nothing to do with??

Also me:  Practically healthy to have the non-choc.

Me:        Should never have opened these stupid emails. I hate my phone.

Also me:  Who is the bastard who buys pain au chocolat anyway?

Me:        If I ever lost my phone, I would probably cease to exist in any form.

Also me:  Thinking about it, they don't have that much chocolate in them anyway. Really stingy, actually. The French are unbelievable.

Me:        Just going to quickly check Instagram as this bit is irrelevant to me. I LOVE MY PHONE.

Also me:  If I eat it and then don't have lunch, then it's fine.

Me:        Wait, why is she talking about Mexico? When did she go to Mexico? How many holidays can one person have in a year?

Also me:  Or a salad for lunch. Just no bread.

Me:      And she's wearing the dress I wanted from Matches.

Also me:  OK, I could have a sandwich, as long as it's, like, gluten-free seeded spelt bread.

Me:      How can she afford that dress? She's a freelancer FFS.

Also me:  YES – someone has taken the croissant, I'M LEGIT GOING IN FOR THE CHOC.

Me:      I wish I were a freelancer. They just sit around all day looking at Facebook and taking naps.

Also me:  OK, don't just leave it sitting on your plate. I can't start eating mine until you start eating yours.

Me:      Maybe starting my own business was a mistake.

Also me:  Stop fingering it. I AM DYING HERE.

Me:      I can't believe I'm supposedly senior to these people. I still mime to Salt-N-Pepa in the mirror.

Also me:  I am starving to death. This must be what it feels like to be a Victoria's Secret Angel...

Me:      And as I take a bite, I'm asked a question. Thank you, forces of evil.

## Confronta-Phobia

So here you are and it's 3am and you are not sleeping. Instead you are mentally agonising over having to have an awkward conversation with someone. In your head it's going something like this:

'Hi X, please sit down. Thank you for this report, but it needs a bit of a tweak. My helpful and brilliant suggestions are here in red. Can I have it back on the desk of my enormous office ASAP?' This is the first fantasy version of this conversation. And then things take a darker turn and you imagine it this way:

'Hi X, [Thinks to self: is X looking rather aggressive?] thank you for this report but...' And suddenly X is throwing an ergonomic chair at you, and walking out, complaining to HR and...

And it being 3am, you sit in this hell loop for the next three hours, having the fantastical fight over and over again with all the, 'You can't handle the truth' and 'Maybe you should take a long hard look at yourself', until you drag your sorry carcass out of bed and into the office to attempt 'the conversation' while over-caffeinated and genuinely traumatised.

Why is it that even a fantasy fight feels so unbelievably precarious these days? As teenagers, the fantasy bust-ups were almost fun – we were so tough in our heads and our combat pants, endlessly slaying adversaries with our imagined withering put-downs. Now the outcome of the fantasy fight, particularly if it's with a lover, is always abandonment. The pre-drawn conclusion is that someone is going to get up and leave forever.

Can we risk a confrontation? Will it go the way we planned? Should we even be planning? Maybe we will just say nothing. Reduced to seething inwardly. Tip-toeing around situations we feel uncomfortable in, scared to be the bitch or bossy.

Well, if you do find yourself in one of those 'situations', here are four thoughts on how to give criticism:

1. Say it face to face. Yes, an email is tempting. But it is easily misinterpreted and a bit cowardly. Are you that person? No.
2. Easy on the 'buts'. There is a theory that 'but' cancels out everything that precedes it. If you must 'but', put the bad stuff first: 'This is not working yet but it will be brilliant.'
3. Push the positive. Try to avoid negging and offer solutions.
4. Practise. And no we don't mean in the shower/3am zone. With an actual real-life friend. We know. Exhausting.

# 20 Signs It's Time To Leave Your Job

1. You check your horoscope every morning longing for it to talk about new opportunities.
2. You pore over those 'Come and look after this small island in the Hebrides/South Pacific' adverts.
3. You didn't go to the Christmas party. You did not have any other plans. You just couldn't be arsed.
4. You passively aggressively cc irrelevant people in the company just to entertain yourself – 'What do you think Jim?', 'Love to know your thoughts on this one Anya…' It annoys everyone. You don't care.
5. You have a YouTube video of Channing Tatum dancing open all day. Every day.
6. You wake up crying on Mondays, Tuesdays, Wednesdays and Thursdays.
7. When you do a coffee run you secretly order decaffeinated coffee for those you don't like. Or full-caff for those who don't want it. Good luck sleeping tonight, Miriam! Ha!
8. You become an expert in under-managing; you say things like 'I favour a hands-off approach' or 'Do whatever the fuck you like'.
9. You pretend that you've started smoking again just to go for fag breaks.
10. You change your boss's ringtone on your phone so that you always know it's them calling and it is the theme from *Jaws*.

11. Your dead father is always ill.
12. You consider blocking out the Glastonbury holiday slots next year just to annoy the millennials in the office.
13. You pray for train strikes/snow/any kind of industrial-scale disruption.
14. You've started adjusting everyone's chairs when you are alone in the office.
15. You've ordered cannabis oil to 'help you sleep' but actually to see if it might also 'help you get through the day'.
16. When someone gets sick you are jealous. When someone comes in sick you practically drink from their coffee cup/lick their water bottle when no one is looking.
17. You buy an office blanket and drape it over your lap at all times, including meetings.
18. You spend hours in the disabled loo on Instagram or snoozing.
19. You consider unionising the office to annoy the higher-ups.
20. You've put on a stone misery-eating at Pret.

## Adventures In Insomnia: Money Worries

INT. A suburban bedroom.
Deep, dark night. An incredibly young-looking woman is in bed. Her pyjamas are distressed. There may be dribble. Cue brain.

Brain:    Squeak, squeak.
Me:       (wakes up panicking) Oh my Christ, what the hell is that?
Brain:    You. Church mouse. (evil laugh)
Me:       What?
Brain:    As in 'poor as a...'
Me:       Thanks for raising this at 2.45am.
Brain:    Incredible that you have been able to sleep for two hours when you HAVE NO MONEY.
Me:       Right, we're not doing this now.
Brain:    Literally the most casual person I have ever met.
Me:       Actually that's—
Brain:    '*Got no money AT ALL, but that can wait until morning.*' You're hilarious.
Me:       Bit over the top, isn't it?
Brain:    Is it, though? Should the bankrupt be allowed to sleep?
Me:       Look, hang on, I'm not—
Brain:    How are you going to pay the mortgage?

| Me: | With the money that I am earning. That I will be earning. Soon. |
| Brain: | DENIALDENIALDENIAL |
| Me: | What do you want from me??? |
| Brain: | A cardboard box for a start – for us both to live in when we lose EVERYTHING. |
| Me: | That won't happen…Will it? |
| Brain: | Don't expect to ever go on holiday again. Or buy any new clothes. Or food. And when was your car last serviced? |
| Me: | I don't know. |
| Brain: | Of course you don't. It's probably dangerous to drive by now. All because you can't pay for the most basic safety checks. |
| Me: | I'll walk everywhere! |
| Brain: | Won't be able to afford the shoes, don't bother. |
| Me: | Think about something else, think about something else. |
| Brain: | I know, pensions! |

# 10 Steps To Self-Employment

Before you read this, we want to be totally honest with you. There is nothing practical here. It's not about taxes or Companies House or how to introduce yourself as an entrepreneur. It's the emotional stuff – the feelings, instincts, all of that. Is a part of you suspicious that PAYE isn't the way forward? Here are the ten stages of jacking it all in…

1. Your first thought in the morning is, 'Oh, not again.'
2. You realise you've got skills. People like you. This makes the company you work for money. But weirdly, does not make you much money. Hmmm…
3. Your stress levels peak. Perhaps you leave the house wearing two different shoes. Forget to put on a bra. Call your husband Peter (when his name is Simon. Which begs the question, 'Who the hell is Peter?'). You've no idea what you're achieving. It's definitely not wealth or self-respect.
4. BREAKTHROUGH: 'What if I did this – or something else – for myself?'
5. The seed is planted. It's the beginning of the end for you and PAYE. Oh God.
6. You tell someone you're going to leave and do your own thing. Now you definitely have to do it.
7. Suddenly PAYE seems absurd. You're an adult but someone tells you when to eat lunch? You're an adult but someone else tells you where to sit all day? I mean, that's weird, right?
8. BREAKTHROUGH: 'I want to do [insert dream]. This is how I'm going to do it.'

This is you, talking out loud to a friend, husband, boyfriend, your mother. Basically someone you trust who has probably, at some point, had a conversation with you while peeing.

9. You hand in your notice. People ask where you're going. You reply, 'To do my own thing.' Colleagues are jealous. Some of them are a bit mean. It is brilliant.

10. DAY ONE: Exhilaration, fear, determination. PAYE is over. Life begins again.

# How To Have An Argument
# When You Know You're Right

How good are you at arguing? Presumably, as you are, like us, living in the 'time-poor/cash-strapped/why is everyone so leisurely' rush hour of our lives, you like your debates short and sweet. Rather than in the realms of EU debates. Or those American filibusters. Put it this way, anything that involves loo breaks is too long. And this is especially true when you are right. You are probably always right.

So here is how to argue with your husband/mother/boss/the person at the checkout in Sainsbury's when you know you're right, about anything and everything.

- Don't try to convince the other person you are right. EVEN THOUGH YOU ARE RIGHT.
- The best thing to do when you're in a position of power is to listen. YOU HAVE THE POWER BY VIRTUE OF BEING RIGHT.
- You are powerful when present, in control and in the moment. ESPECIALLY BECAUSE YOU ARE RIGHT.
- Give the other person the chance to speak their side. RIGHT RIGHT RIGHT.
- This will allow them to feel like they are being heard. THOUGH THE FACT REMAINS: STILL RIGHT.
- Listen closely and find out why the person is really upset. THEY MAY BE UPSET BECAUSE THEY ARE WRONG. AND YOU ARE RIGHT.
- You might be surprised what's really bothering them and gain new insight into your relationship. HANG ON, WEREN'T WE TALKING ABOUT YOU BEING RIGHT?

No one said it was easy to be right. But actually, this should be the perfect opportunity for a bit of mental relaxation, a little meditation. Because you are right. Right?

# Chapter 7

# IT'S NOT ME, IT'S YOU

WHY IS IT, IN THIS ENLIGHTENED AGE, that 'single', with all its freedom and opportunity, retains the suggestion of pity? Maybe it's the word. It implies being left: 'still single'. There's no active choice inferred by 'remaining single'. We are all born single and single we stay until we are chosen. Alone. A problem waiting to be solved.

What if we could change up the conversation a little? What if, when people ask, 'Are you married?' or the mindlessly spiteful, 'Did you never marry?' we could answer, 'No. I'm independent.' Or, imagine if those curious types were to frame and phrase their probing differently and ask, 'Are you in a couple or are you independent?'

It might allow women to move on from the unplucked flower narrative of millennia. We are born single but we are not born independent. We learn and we earn that. It is proudly won. Why can't independence be recognised as the collateral gain of the lone voyager? Language is atmospheric. It has the power to refresh, to give small girls an alternative scenario to visualise, beyond the white dress: the adventurer, the explorer, the self-determiner. After all, it's a journey, not a predicament.

That's all fine and good and right and proper but being independent doesn't mean we don't yearn. We yearn. And we don't yearn any less at 40 than we did at 18. Maybe we yearn more. We definitely yearn differently. And, often, privately. And, sometimes, shamefully. Aloneness flirts with loneliness. Anticipation veers towards panic. And so we try to date. We open our hearts to the possibilities and, after every false start, after the disappointment leaves us momentarily breathless, then we put ourselves back together and we try again. Because there is a narcotic aspect to dating – why do you think dating apps are so addictive when only 5 per cent of people meet their partners online? The next swipe might be him. The next set-up might be him. Will he be at this party, that conference, the other pub? Oh yes, of course, he'll turn up when I'm least expecting him. So here I am, monumentally unexpectant…on I go…where the fuck is he? I'm exhausted.

Dating for grown-ups is a horror story. Not because of the anecdotal evidence that there isn't much out there and what there is might be majorly dysfunctional. Not because we are scared of looking desperate. Not because all the past traumas and disappointments have concertinaed up on us to make us incredibly bruisable. Not because we are worried about our bodies and our sexual athleticism, audacity and appetite. All of the above is dealable with. Intimidating, sure, but processable.

No, dating for grown-ups is a nightmare because we have never really done it. When we were getting our sea-legs, 'dating' was still an Americanism. If you were dating, in England, in the Nineties and Noughties, then you probably weren't really dating at all. You may have dived in and out of liaisons and flings and relationships, but it was not a *Sex and the City*, 'Tonight I've got a date with a hot lawyer/pilot/gallerist' situation.

The way that we interviewed, in our twenties and early thirties, was to get almost insensibly drunk and fall on top of each other. Maybe numbers were swapped. Maybe numbers were texted or even called…imagine that! But the first date certainly came after the first snog and possibly after the first shag. Fluids, then first dates. Was it as icky as it sounds? Sometimes. But sometimes it ended in marriage.

So these days, when we maybe don't quite get so steamingly pissed; when we might be a little more circumspect with our bodies; when we need to turn up for drinks or dinner with a prospective lover…well, we are babies. Scared babies. In heels. 'Just be yourself,' say the married people. 'Who knows, you might make a new friend.' Oh, how quickly they forget…

They forget about the contradiction implicit in protecting your heart from too, too, too much pain and simultaneously safe-guarding your vulnerability because beautiful things happen in vulnerable spaces. Creativity, joy, love spring out of vulnerability. Opening our hearts and letting someone see us is the true challenge. And going on an actual date is, in itself, a clear statement of vulnerability. It says 'I am here and I hope…' That is the challenge. That is the terror. And that is the magic. Do not cower because you are solo. Do not pretend. Be wholehearted. Be proud. And onwards…

# Things You Only Know If You're Single Over 35

## Married Women Can't Decide…

if you are pathetic or dangerous. Nor can married men. Married women think they are being inclusive when they ask you to coffee after a dinner party (singles bugger up the numbers) and often sit you next to another woman as 'punishment'.

## Unless A Man Is…

gay, married or dead you have to fancy him or you will endure a chorus of 'See???? You are impossibly picky. You have to learn to compromise.' No matter that he clearly has a personality disorder/a drug habit/is in prison. The problem, my friends, is yours. You: 'He beat up his ex-wife.' Friend: 'People change.'

## When People Call You Brave…

it is not a compliment. It is because they are horrified by your predicament. You may well not be horrified. You may well be basking in the peace/freedom. But they are still horrified.

### You Are Amazed By How Many Relationships...

you don't envy. Sure, there are a few (usually counted on one hand) that look like fun and solace rolled up into one lovely partnership. But most look like hard bloody work without much reward.

### Men Don't Care...

if you have cellulite. Or wrinkles. Believe it. They don't. If they do then you are aiming low and missing. You are no longer a trophy – these days you are a prize. You haven't waited this long to just...settle.

### Endless Questions And Calculations...

If I am 42 and I meet him at 43 and he is 48, then how much sex can we cram in before everything dries up or flops? Do I even have the energy? Where will I put him? Everything will be OK but what does OK look like? Am I free or am I tragic? Am I desperate or am I powerful? Does everyone secretly think I'm a lesbian? What if he never appears? What then? What does that mean? Babies! Babies? Babies...Oh God, stepchildren.

## Someone Else Is Married To My Husband

The ones that get away are, generally, not the ones we love and lose. The ones that get away are the ones we never truly know. They are a fleeting thing; a memory so brief that it renders itself entirely mouldable. I've had a few husbands, you see, who I never married. Or even kissed. But, in some imaginary hinterland that harms no one, they are mine. Would you like to meet one?

There we find ourselves, attached only by our eye beams tangling across this crowded room. Slowly but determinedly we snake and ladder our way towards each other while the night is still so, so young. We find a corner. Well, it feels like a corner but it is in full view, above board, irreproachable. He is married. He is the marrying kind. He is after nothing except the next moment, laugh, flash, fix, bolt. I am enraptured. No risk, nothing to win or lose but just fully inside the moment. 'Be present,' they say, 'be mindful.' For once I am present but mindless. My mind is blown.

Others come and go as the party peaks and troughs; we invite them into our nook. It is both an opportunity to show off a little, to create immediate in-jokes and to ensure that proceedings are utterly, publicly legit.

He is perfection, this man. He can be perfection, you see, because however close he feels, he is remote; a distant oasis of possibility in a desert, a jungle, an ocean of doubt and...hope?

He mentions his wife enough to set the boundaries. I ask about her enough to reinforce them. Nothing is going to happen. We probably won't swap numbers using work as an excuse. If I want to see him again I'll invite them to something as a couple, I suppose. Just to take another look. To work out if someone else is married to my husband. Because today, tonight, right now and for a day or two afterwards, that's exactly how it feels. And I will find a way to live with that. Just as I did last time and the time before.

## Tinder: Terrifying Or Tantalising?

Let's have a little word about online dating shall we? Hang on – don't panic, don't go all defensive and 'it's just not for me' because you're terrified. Likelihood is, it's fear that's activating that knee-jerk repulsion but it's fine if it manifests as irritability. I know that one.

So we're all grown-ups and we know who we know, right? Maybe your people are excellent at doing set-ups. Mine aren't. Maybe you wheel about the place chanting, 'Know anyone single and not a dick?' into the void. Don't blame your friends – they're as tired and preoccupied as you are and maybe you have a bit too much texture to make for an easy fit. I know that one too.

But that doesn't mean you can't be in the game.

Because if online dating – and by that I mean Tinder – is good for one thing it is this: it activates your antennae. It gets you looking again. As a participant not a spectator.

And if it is good for another thing, it's practice. Harmless flirtation. Hone it. Dial it up, dial it down. They come and they go and you learn that – in the early stages – it doesn't matter. You learn that their reaction to you is not information about you but about them.

It's a bit fast food, making everyone seem a little disposable, but it's a game. To get you back in the game. And the world will notice the smile on your face, the swing in your step. A date a month rather than a date a year. Just popping on to the app to have a little browse reminds you that there are possibilities. And possibility is a higher power...

# Conversations You Have With Yourself On A Date

Me:        He's hot.
Also me:  Is he though?
Me:        He's tall.
Also me:  Shorter than my last two boyfriends.
Me:        Good teeth.
Also me:  Serial killer shoes. Probably chosen by his mother.
Me:        Nice laugh.
Also me:  Sounds a bit like Barbara Windsor?
Me:        He thinks I'm funny.
Also me:  He's laughing at me.
Me:        It's nice that he has a dog.
Also me:  The dog will watch us having sex and he won't mind.
Me:        He's very complimentary.
Also me:  He just wants to get laid.
Me:        Can I order the steak? Will it make me look greedy?
Also me:  OMG, don't attempt sex on a full stomach, you fool.
Me:        I think I'll just play it cool this time.
Also me:  I want to marry him.
Me:        He's suitably outraged about the NRA.
Also me:  When is it OK to change the subject to *Game of Thrones*?
Me:        He probably doesn't have time to watch much TV.
Also me:  BAD SIGN, VERY BAD SIGN.
Me:        I'm glad I brought up North Korea.
Also me:  Do I have spinach in my teeth?
Me:        He's easy to talk to.
Also me:  I haven't waxed.
Me:        I will stick to my feminist principles and pay half.
Also me:  If he doesn't offer to pay the whole thing, he's an arsehole.
Me:        He's offering to drop me home. Result.
Also me:  I left my knickers drying on the clothes rack in my bedroom!!
Me:        Excited about all the sex that's about to happen.
Also me:  How do I get away with watching *Strictly* on Catch Up first?

# The Trouble With Gentlemen Callers

What manner of medieval throwback is this? Picture the scene: you are single. You went to a dinner thing last night and there was an amusing man there and you don't know if you'd be up for anything with him (these days your wires are so short-circuited that you have to suck it and see, really) but you kind of had more fun than you've had in a while. And you were surprisingly yourself. So that was all in all rather edifying. And maybe you'll bump into him someday, somewhere, and even if you don't it's all good practice. So that's all good.

Anyway, you are on your way to the station/shrink/gym and your phone rings and you don't recognise the number, but it doesn't look like one of those dodgy ones so you answer it with a curt hello and you hear, 'Name? Hi, this is NAME. From last night…'

Oh dear God, just when we are coming to terms with Tinder and WhatsApp and sexting and new-gen romance, men have decided to go all retro and postmodern and pick up the damn phone. What to say? Who has time? Is my voice OK? Should we be making a plan? This is a nightmare.

We grown-up women are monumentally out of practice when it comes to the phone chat. So, if you get a caller, start calling your friends again to flex the phone muscle; to work out which jokes work when body language is not available. If you only talk to your mother on the phone your instinct will be completely off. Oh, and for the uninitiated, our research shows that the ideal length (!) is about 15 minutes. And you need to be the one to call time. And don't talk so much that you become phone pals. And don't have phone sex before you have actual sex. And make sure he calls you more than you call him. Some things never change. But, put simply, if a man calls you it is a very, very good sign.

# Never Ask A Married

Married people should never be consulted about romantic conundrums. They are hopeless. How quickly they forget the need to be nuanced and yet direct. You know that incredibly early embryonic stage where you may or may not have drunkenly kissed but you have not yet had a date and you are tentatively texting and trying to get your tone of voice right? Faintly flirty but absolutely backtrackable. Green light-ish but dignified. Amusing yet…potentially a keeper. Responding in a timely fashion; not too keen yet not game-playery. Balance. Sass. Measure.

Married people say things like, 'Just text him and tell him you're not wearing any knickers. That'll work.' Work for what? They want to read every text, which is deeply unnerving because they have also forgotten that it is CRUCIAL not to text anything by mistake so they are careless with your phone. They want every detail to remind them of skirmishes that aren't all, 'Have you emptied the dishwasher?' Married people tend also to be extremists, either hopelessly romantic – 'He loves you!' – or deeply cynical – 'They are all liars.' Neither is helpful.

Married people want the best for you in a kind of spectator sport way. They are rooting for you but they can in no way walk a mile in your single shoes. And so, when it comes to sex and romance, turn to the singles; they feel the frisson. They are in touch with the jeopardy and the possibility. The married people – bless them – are little more than giggling loons.

## The Anatomy Of A Midult Crush

### Mentionitis
Suddenly you need to urgently communicate everything the crush has ever said to everyone you have ever met. 'Frank' thinks that curtains are overrated. 'Frank' thinks that Mercury going into retrograde has no effect on anyone. 'Frank' thinks that you should clean your windows once a month to keep your house bright. You have mentionitis. You think no one notices. You are wrong.

### Funny Face
Not helped by that weird look on your face. Like an invisible plastic surgeon is pulling some facelift strings tight and your mouth is twitching in a most erratic way. If we were French we would call it 'a certain smile'[†] but we're aware that you look most suspicious. Your best friends keep saying, 'What is wrong with your face?'

### Distraction Addiction
Already you are struggling in the concentration department, already it is hard enough to keep focused on what Mike from Acquisitions is mansplaining today, and it's taken 1,001 nights to read this book because you keep falling asleep with it on your face. But to heap Pelion on Ossa you are now daydreaming about the crush so vividly that you missed your cunting bus stop.

### Hot Stuff
Hand in hand with the Midult crush is wild purchasing. Stuff for the life you are fantasising about, not the life you lead. Why do hold-ups suddenly feel like a good idea? A silk shirt that you can be suggestively impeccable in, even though you don't own an iron? Did you really just do a trying-on session in Agent Provocateur?

---

[†] *Un certain sourire*, you know, lit from within like a mysterious French girl about to be 'discovered' in the *tabac*. Except you are not French or mysterious and you look really quite weird and smirky.

**Blindness**

All your deal-breakers are…broken. And yet onwards the fantasy marches. Terrible teeth, weirdly tiny hands, squeaky nasal voice, intellectual snobbery, bad breath, a truly bizarre relationship with his mother. Once the crush veil has fallen over your eyes, he is a god and you worship at the altar of his…wait, is one arm shorter than the other?

**Crush Shame**

Then just as quickly as it, ahem, came, the door in your head slams and the feeling has passed. Midiotic romantic notions always, always, always pass (the exceptions are so few and far between that we do not take them into account). And it is like you have been freed from a spell, and you think, what the fuck was that? And you are probably a bit ashamed. But don't be.

# If There's One Thing Men Hate…

Not long ago, the most repellent words a woman can use on an online dating profile were 'revealed'. Ta-dah! This is the stuff that really puts men off. Brace yourselves. Violent? Nope. Mentally unstable? Nope. Alcoholic? Nope. Articulate? Yup, that's apparently the passion killer. God forbid we should be able to have a conversation. Or, actually, does the crime lie in the horribly self-aggrandising assertion that we judge ourselves able to have a conversation? How absolutely dare we put our verbal dexterity on the table? Every man online has apparently just gone limp at the thought that one of us might be able to tell an amusing story. Or provide an insight of any kind. Every man will start vomiting if you keep saying how articulate you are. Just ugh. Honestly.

The sexiest word? Ambitious. Quite right. Focused, driven, powerful women are profoundly and enrichingly attractive. But, listen: if a man can't handle a woman able to express herself or tell a joke, then he doesn't want ambition. What he wants to check is that a woman will go Dutch and won't be any kind of financial drain. Ever. If we dared to articulate this further, we'd assume that he needs to know that she isn't a 'gold-digger'. And, while we're here, one man was roundly shamed by a dating app recently after he called women 'entitled, gold-digging whores' when a potential date asked him about his job. Weeding out gold-diggers may be fair enough but it's a world (and a word) away from finding ambition an actual turn-on. After all, ambitious women will tend to be reasonably…articulate.

Incidentally, want to know the biggest turn-on for women? Is it rich? Nope. Powerful? Nope. Physically fit. Check us out. We know what we want.

# How To Make Contact

Maybe it's party season. Anyway, you've met someone you connected with. And then you panicked and ran away without swapping numbers or establishing any kind of plan. You are 80 per cent sure that he felt the connection too. There are two things you need to know here. It's one thing saying that the universe will provide and you should leave these things to fate. It's another thing to be a Midult and remember that fate may not have your mobile number.

Here's how to make contact:

1.   Calm down. There's nothing at stake yet. You are perfectly safe.
2.   Ask a witness if it was just you. Were you chasing him round the dance floor/pub? Was he materialising at your side every five seconds? This needs to be a witness you trust. Not a friend who loves a bit of drama.
3.   Wrestle his number off a mutual friend/the internet/a private detective. Avoid messaging on social media. At all costs. It's just murky.

You now have two choices. Either make like you are 15 and get someone to organise a games night/dinner/gathering and ensure he is invited. Or text him yourself and say something like: 'Hello X. This is Y.' (There is no need to say 'from the other night'. If he says 'Who?' the connection was in your head or he is a bit of dick. Either way better to know now.)

To continue…'Hello X. This is Y. It was great to meet you the other night. x' (Yes, with a kiss.)

You don't need to suggest a meeting or do anything else at all. You've very firmly taken the bull by the horns and now you are putting the ball back in the bull's court. Simple. Direct. Now forget about it. Ha!

# Dear Dick Pic…

'No disrespect to all you penises out there,' is probably how we ought to open this conversation. You very much have a role in our lives. You are important and capable of bringing much joy and entertainment. You can be funny, you can be clever, you can be flattering – in fact, if your conversation were better, you could sort of be like the ideal man in some ways, which is confusing. But – and don't take this the wrong way – aesthetically you are *looks at the ceiling and not at you* challenging. Not when you're attached to your owner if that owner is someone we are keen on. But by yourself. Disassociated. In a dick pic. Which is basically like a passport photo. And that passport photo has somehow ended up on my phone and I'm supposed to feel pleased about it. Or, even more unlikely, aroused. This is separate to you being arousing as an entity – you are, don't get paranoid – and of course beauty is in the eye of the beholder. It's just when you pop up on my iPhone screen, straining and eager in a non-contextualised environment, you fall short of your goals. The picture becomes about something else – your shape, your proportions, your…colour. It's all a bit silly. Or a bit aggressive. A bit gratuitous. Sorry. And your purpose gets lost, which is a shame. You are either mildly horrifying or deeply hilarious. And this is even before we've got to the whole testicle situation, which does not improve things, sadly.

Don't be disheartened. You still have many strengths. It's just you're not a solo artist. You should not attempt a career on your own. No eponymous albums, please. You need a band, an entourage, a support system, i.e. a man to be stuck to at all times. Who we can see. Remember, you are loved and respected. Most of the time. Now, make yourself useful and become a bit camera shy. We'd appreciate it.

## Welcome to Midulthood

# WHAT MIDULTS HATE HEARING

1. Your bag is overweight.
2. Do you even know how much sugar there is in that apple?
3. I think you've had enough.
4. Can I have a word?
5. School reunion!!!!!!!!
6. What a shame.
7. Our engineer should be with you between 5am and 10pm.
8. Please continue to hold, your call is important to us.
9. I am thinking of organising a long weekend in Ibiza for my birthday this year.
10. Shall we go camping?
11. Where have you put Dad's ashes?
12. Are we still on for tonight?
13. We don't have Wi-Fi here so you can completely switch off!
14. Ooh, that looks comfortable.
15. The specific crumple of an empty packet of crisps/biscuits.
16. I'm not looking for anything serious.
17. Unexpected item in the bagging area.
18. First of all, you need to deal with that pigmentation.
19. This never happened with my wife.

## Chapter 8

# EXCUSE ME, WHAT LEVEL OF HELL IS THIS?

PERHAPS EVERYONE COULD EASE OFF telling grown-up people that we are the new grey and it really doesn't matter that we're not the new black anymore because we can still be relevant (to our newly grey peers, at least) in some small, cosy, face-creamy kind of a way. If 60 is the new 40, then 40 is the new fuck off. Anti-ageing is a mad, bad and dangerous phrase because, unless you have a time machine in your handbag, nestling among the lidless lipsticks, hairballs and stray bits of gum, it's not possible. It suggests that ageing is an illness. Or an avoidable condition. Actually, ageing is a privilege. But that doesn't mean it's comfortable.

Age is the space in the middle of the personal Venn diagram where time meets change. And, oh yes, we change. Does this feel familiar:

> *I look tired. Bags. I've never had bags before; always been lucky like that. So this puffy, shadowy situation must be because I am tired. Except, oddly, I am not really tired. And something is happening around my jawline. So, clearly I must be retaining water. And have my eyes got just a tiny bit…smaller? Is that even possible? And my body is different. I want to say fatter, but the scales read the same and my clothes fit the same but they don't look the same. They hang…otherly. As though someone else is wearing them. The thing is, I just don't look like myself. Not the self I have become accustomed to.*

This is disorientating and tough stuff. Still you…but not you? Waiting for things to revert and knowing that they won't. It isn't that you suddenly have a full beard, deep crow's feet and a vast tyre of spread. But it is a hint of what is to come. This is your face now. Who knows how long you have to get used to this physical self before it shifts once more. Shift happens. Inevitability is a strange beast.

Once upon a time youth was an island and, when you voyaged away from that pimply atoll, you no longer had any access to its preconceptions, its obsessions, dysfunctions and amusements. But that was in a pre-tech era, where the definition of hyper-connectivity was one of those hideous chain letters (pass this on and you'll get rich, ignore it and you'll die horribly) that plonked onto the doormat. Now, we can see what teenagers are looking at, listen to the music, Google the vocabulary, marvel at the sheer speed with which culture writhes and thrashes. It is dawning on the world that grown-up women may not just be 'busy working mums' or 'cougars'. This is a demographic without borders – it evolves as it ages. It doesn't check out. It remains in discovery mode. Our age is no longer signposted by our interests. We are not exclusively Googling insulation, vacuum cleaners and arch supports. We are the ones buying Topshop sunglasses: we just can't bear to lose another pair of 200 pounders because it makes us feel like such tools. We are the ones downloading The Stormzy[†]: we need something to work out to that isn't the *Rocky* theme tune. We are the ones buying the Adidas Superstars but, now you come to mention it, they might be for our 73-year-old mother's birthday (because 74 is the new up yours). Research is compelling, data is beautiful, but prescriptive pigeon-holing is boring and inaccurate. It is true that, until very recently, the difference between generations was immediately obvious from the clothes, the language, the point of view. But, today, that slicing up of mindsets feels like a relic, and an artificial one at that. Our skin may tell a story, but our brains can roam free from those silly labels. It comes down to relevance. And relevance is readily available if we choose to pay attention. Choose to stay engaged.

In one life, we have myriad incarnations. The very young assume that everyone else has somehow switched off. That their blinkers are on and their synapses are dulled and they are wearing emotion-cancelling headphones for the soul. That we care less, mean less, are less. The opposite is true but practice makes perfect. We've been feeling all that stuff for decades and we're just...better at it. Unless things go wonky (and, certainly, they threaten to often enough) maturity can just lead to a more efficient processing system, so the wiser of the elders will often appear more contained. Why waste energy on flailing about? Because, truly, age is an opportunity to get better at being you.

## All The Girls We've Been

### The Summertime Slut

Remember that phase? You were maybe 28, and you broke up with your boyfriend and were absolutely floored with the heartbreak. Oof, even just thinking about it hurts. And you lost so much weight, and suddenly it was summer and you went on a festival of fucks and that didn't really help either.

### The Fashion Phenomenon

The day you woke up and decided to be a fashion-forward sensation. It was a Tuesday. You went to Harvey Nichols and you spent 10,000 million pounds (approx.) on a

---

[†] We know it's Stormzy but this is what they think of us, isn't it? They think we call our laptops 'the machine'.

cream Céline coat that you have never worn. Because it cost more than your flat and it makes you look like a fridge. Every now and then you get it out and think what might have been…It's probably time to sell it.

## The Surrendered Girlfriend
He was a total shit but, you know, maybe that was your destiny. I mean, your father was an arsehole. So yes, it was OK when he whined about the size of your bum, or refused to pick you up from the station when you went to visit him in the arse-end of nowhere, or shouted at you because he didn't like the way you washed up. It's taken years and many £££ to get over the fact that you went out with him at all.

## The Terrible Employee
The permanently late for work, the booze breath, the forgetting to send faxes or not even bothering to answer the phone, let alone taking a message. The not showing up at all. And if you had to show up, you could be found having a nap under the desk, when you weren't sending out CVs. Not forgetting the fag breaks and the loud booking of Brazilian waxes over the phone.

## The Shadow
The time when you were so unhappy, so in the wilderness, that you didn't really exist.

## The Yogi
You had a weird gardening leave thingy for a few weeks so decided to take up yoga – you booked a class pass at a centre. Maybe it was a hot one. After the first class you were so enlightened, so in the zone, that you start Googling retreats in the UK and spent a fortune at Lululemon. After the second, you decide to bypass the UK and go straight for an India swami for a more authentic experience. During the third class you hurt your knee and never went back.

## The Weekday Binge Drinker
This phase lasted 20 years and then suddenly you woke up and it was a nightmare and you had crossed the hangover Rubicon and now you can only have two units a week.

## The Power Dresser

You got your first office job and after three months of earning and hanging on by the seat of your Topshop trousers you decided to be a grown-up. So you went to Joseph and bought a pinstripe suit. You still have the jacket – ¾ length, double-breasted, wide lapels, small shoulder pads. It's surely coming back in style ANY MOMENT NOW.

## The Cool Haircut Person

You had medium-length brown hair forever. Was it your hair holding you back from being the cool, relevant gal you knew you were on the inside? You went to a salon and told them to give you a 'cool haircut'. Your mother said, 'You're going to need to wear a lot more make-up now.' You cried for what felt like years.

## The Fresh Executive

It's your first job without 'assistant' in the title. This is IT. You are IT. The past is in the past, no more coming in late, going to festivals every weekend and returning to the office/Earth swivel-eyed with dirty hair. You eat weird sushi for lunch and go into Jigsaw and finger all the navy trousers.

## The Break-Up Denier

So the reason he hasn't phoned for two weeks is that he is on holiday in the South of France (nothing strange there) and he has accidentally tripped and fallen into a well and is trapped. That's why you keep phoning to see if he's OK and that's why he's not calling you back. Shame. (My heart still slightly breaks for this girl.)

## The Addict-Lite

It's completely normal to not be able to leave the house without a shot of vodka, right? And to not be able to sleep without taking something: Benadryl, Xanax, anti-histamine, Night Nurse. I mean, who sleeps? No one sleeps. And we are all anxious as anything, so what if we need a little crutch/sharpener every now and then? And no, you didn't drink all two bottles of rosé while watching *Sex and the City*. It's summer and it's hot; there was loads of ice in your glass. Everything is fine. You are fine. *shivers*

## The Escapologist

You are done with towns. You are done with London. If you have to sit on the Underground for one more minute going to a job that you hate, you will scream. *thinks to self, 'When was I last happy?'* Dimly remembers a time when you went to Dorset and went crabbing (you were seven). You were happy then. So you hit Zoopla hard. 'Look at that creamy cottage with the lilac and the orchard. I could be happy again.' You do nothing. (Unless you do.)

### The Lust Lunatic
Yes he's short/bald/obnoxious/bit of a dick. But oh my God the sex. The sex. You cannot think straight. You just want to have sex with him. All the time. Can't remember your own name/friends/pets/responsibilities/moral code. Can't do anything but have sex. You are lit by a SEX FIRE. Until *La Repulsion* (that feeling of utter, irreversible revulsion) suddenly descends. Some people call it *The Ick*. Maybe you were in an ill-advised candle-lit bath with him at the time. Whatever. And just like that you are free. The fire is out.

### The Artful Juggler
Everything in your life was colour-coded and filed and organised. The drawers were tidy, even the secret random ones. You were nailing work, your personal life seemed to be fully functioning, you made things like meringues and chicken pie. You walked out of the house looking clean and sane every single day. Your bra fitted. What an amazing week that was.

### The Vanisher
One day you were there, at the parties, the work drinks, all the social things, the library protests, the openings, the everythings. The next you had vanished, stopped going out, stopped returning calls. You just...went another way. 'I thought you were dead,' said someone jokingly at a party the other day. Maybe you were a bit.

### The Nun
When you stopped having sex. For two years at least. You are not even sure why it happened. Or why it started up again. Has it?

### The Appalling Decision Maker
Remember the time when you lost your radar and your instinct and your gut feeling and developed idiot brain and every single decision you made was wrong. You took that job and ended up miserable: exhausted from the commute and the boss who was a terror. You dumped the nice safe guy and went out with an emotional savage who was terrible in bed. You moved in with someone and regretted it immediately. You wore weird clothes. You hated your hair. You hated yourself. You were trapped in your seriously poor judgement for at least a year. It haunts you. It could happen again.

**The Pirate**

You fucked who you wanted, drank what you wanted, including all the coffee and all the booze in the world. You didn't give a shit about laundry or socks, you danced all night and got on aeroplanes half cut. You smoked with abandon, your clothes were random, you were fantastic. Gaaaaaarhhhhh. It was one summer. One great summer. *buys a pair of pirate boots* *doesn't feel the same* *cries*

# How Did We Become Responsible Members Of Society?

Do you ever get that feeling when you are driving a car and you think, 'Oh my God I am driving a car. When did I become the driver? Why am I always in the front seat?' Or maybe when you lock the front door at night and you think, 'How grown-up am I to be locking my very own door? Should it even be allowed? I am not very responsible really.'

Or you are part of a big, important meeting and throwing around stuff like 'ROI' and 'B2B' and you are like, 'Whoa. It seems only yesterday I was throwing shapes or shots and who knew? Who knew that one day I would have the appearance of a grown-up? With grown-up accoutrements. Who knew, with all the parties and the drugs and the crappy men, that I would one day be responsible for real things?'

Like all of us, I have had my shady moments. Behaved like a dick. Been unreliable or devastated by something. Been almost swallowed by the darkness. At that time, who knew that I would one day be a fully-paid up, committed (rather than sectioned) member of society? Who marches and volunteers and goes climbing at a sports centre at weekends.

You might have a case of the who knews. Hell, you might be walking down the street and looking at a woman walking down the street and thinking, 'There she goes, that reliable individual.' But if you look closer you can see that she is reverberating with her own history, pulsating with her past. You just need to look hard enough.

# Things We Wish We'd Known When We Were 30

1. There is nothing casual about casual sex. It gets to you.
2. Settle for a job (easier to get a gig when you've got a gig) if you're at a loose end but don't settle for a man.
3. Men. If you are chasing him, it means he is running away. This is an exceedingly sobering thought but, now that we are less young and less able to convince ourselves that he just likes us too much to text, it is best kept front of mind.
4. Tears are good for you. But if they don't stop, you need to find help.
5. Promises are broken. It's devastating but it's life. Try to keep yours.

6.  Getting your fertility checked is empowering. Knowledge is choices. Choices are freedom.
7.  Hangovers are just not that bad yet, so stop complaining about them. You wait.
8.  Take care of your skin, you fool. Factor 15 is not high enough. Use fake tan.
9.  If someone suggests you should go out dancing, say yes. One day you'll realise you stopped doing that sort of thing and you won't know how it happened.
10. Take more holidays. Go to far-flung places that might give you food poisoning. Sleep in not very good hotels and make friends with strange foreigners.

## Go On...Take A Year Off

Remember when you mocked those older women who lied about their age? When you truffle hunted for evidence that they were trimming the years off? When you crowed triumphantly at uncovering the untruth. Now hate yourself for a moment. And now forgive yourself. And now let's talk...

Perhaps you have a big birthday in the post. Or any birthday, because they all herald the passing of time. Once you said you would never be so pathetic, so shallow, as to lie about your age but what if you're just not quite ready to be 38 or 40 or 47 or 51? What if you need a little time?

Lie about your age. Do it. Just a year. Stick. As in blackjack. Nothing more for now, thanks ever so much. I'm good. Because if you just shave a year off it acts as a shock absorber. You haven't lopped so much off that your cultural references go skew-whiff. You don't need to lie about where you were when 'Like a Virgin' came out (veering violently backwards from first fag to first steps) and your oldest friends can remain your contemporaries. Just in a slightly looser sense.

One year of grace gives you breathing space. It lets you age gracefully. Let's take 40 as a for instance. Can't face it? Don't do it. Don't turn 40. Hang out in 39 for 12 extra months and by the time your next birthday swings around you'll be delighted to be 40. It'll be like someone has given you a present. 'I'm 40!' you will shout triumphantly – as your inner workings start to chew on the idea of being 41. Works at any age. Works a treat.

# Sophisticated, Experienced, Seasoned...

I'm not agèd. But I'm not in the very first flush. At an excellent age, let's say. But not an age when you welcome other people's comments about where you sit in the age spectrum. And, as I am launching my own business, this has started to happen all the time. Suddenly the language around me has shifted, like the air around me. It's as though my ripeness is being prodded and commented on all the time. And I don't know how I feel about this. It started with my accountant:

'You're going to be fine!' he says.
'Really?' I reply.
'You're not like other entrepreneurs!' he adds.
'Exactly!' I agree, pleased that even he can recognise my uniqueness.
'You're sophisticated,' he says with a nod.

Wait...what? Sophisticated? He panics. Rambles about how most entrepreneurs are ten and that's not always a good thing. But I'm not listening. I'm reeling over the fact someone has just called me not young to my face. Not old. But definitely not young. Is that OK?

Then it happens again. This time with a potential investor.

Him: 'Well the good news is, everyone seems to really like you.'
Me:  'Thanks!'
Him: 'It's because you're experienced. Not an arrogant youngster!'
Me:  'Great!' (frowny face)

Is this a new level of hell to watch out for? Identifying when someone, out of nowhere – when we're not even discussing age – comments on yours without any warning? Also, what do these euphemisms for being not young actually mean? To regain control, we've constructed a six-part guide.
Euphemisms for being not young:

1. Sophisticated. Not young but foxy with it. Still got game. Like Mrs Peacock in Cluedo.
2. Experienced. Good CV. Probably been made redundant and had an office affair at least once.
3. Grown-up. Able to wear a cape with authority. Never gets financially shafted

EXCUSE ME, WHAT LEVEL OF HELL IS THIS?

when the boiler needs fixing.
4.  Responsible. Always giving people lifts. Organises stuff at Christmas. Probably needs a holiday and a haircut.
5.  Worldly. A step beyond experienced. And slightly tarty.
6.  Seasoned. This is just rude.

# Never Say Never

'I shall never, ever kiss a man with a beard.' Me, circa 1997. By 1998 I was deranged over a bearded bear who was almost unrelentingly horrid to me.

'I shall never, ever have Botox.' Also me, circa 2009. By 2011 I was on a six-month rolling appointment cycle with some artful charlatan on Harley Street.

'I shall never, ever get an interest-only mortgage.' Guess who in 2013? And, by 2014, guess what?

'Never' really ought to banned from the grown-up lexicon. Use of it starts to look like idiocy-lite once you've been tossed around a bit and it starts to dawn that dealing in absolutes is delusional. Never saying never runs in direct parallel to the theory that, the more you learn, the less you realise you know.

Absolutes set us up for failure because they are a declaration of permanence. And life, in its essence, isn't permanent. 'Never' sets you up for shame and regret. Why would you do that to yourself?

Here are a few things to never say never about:

- He'll never be unfaithful.
- I'll never have anal sex.
- I'll never take anti-depressants.
- I'll never have plastic surgery.
- I'll never eat refined sugar again.
- I'll never drink again.
- I'll never get a puppy.
- I'll never move to the country.
- I'll never move to the city.
- I'll never get an Alexa.

—151—

# 10 Childhood Punishments That Are Now Treats

You used to think your parents were brutal and insane. Turns out they were actually GENIUSES.

### 1. You Are Not Going To That Party
Not having to stand in a crowded room with people you don't know and music too loud and nowhere to sit and oh, look, there's your ex with his new girlfriend who was born in 1990 and God my feet hurt. Damn.

### 2. You Are Not Leaving The House
You don't have to think about make-up. Or keys. Or taking the car or not taking the car. Or where your phone is and what the weather's like. Shame.

### 3. You Are Going To Bed Early
You are not allowed to stay up and worry about the weird noise the boiler is making. You HAVE to go to bed. Poor you.

### 4. You Are Banned From The Phone
You can't be shouted at by your sister or have lengthy discussions about whether your friend should join Tinder. You don't have to find the moral fibre to not check your emails at midnight or try and work out how you pause Instagram stories because they're just too damn quick to read. Really sad about that.

### 5. Go To Your Room And Read
Lie down on your own with no one asking you questions and read. A book. With a story. In silence. Just you and the bed. And the book. Mmmm, feeling a bit sleepy now. That'll teach you!

### 6. You Have To Be Home By 10pm
You are at a drinks thing you forced yourself to go to because of a duty/FOMO combo and there's all that chat about mortgages and investment properties and sorry, but it's now 9.30 and you HAVE to go because you've got this curfew. Not your fault or your choice.

### 7. Your Boyfriend Has To Sleep In The Spare Room
Oh no. You have to sleep in your own bed. With room to stretch your legs out or switch on the light if you feel like it or thrash about a bit. The temperature isn't volcanic

because of that extra body. You can have the window open if you want. No one is breathing loudly or flinging their jerky arms about. How will you cope?

## 8. Cover Yourself Up

Not allowed to wear that thin dress that looks like it's made of tissue and is flatteringly but uncomfortably tight. Have to wear this cosy jumper instead. Sad to no longer be freezing or anxious about flashing your cellulite when you cross your legs. Really annoyed about this, actually.

## 9. Go And Have A Nap

In the middle of the afternoon? To calm down? That's going to be so unpleasant.

## 10. Do You Want To Be Spanked?

You've been very naughty. Now you're going to find out what happens to naughty girls who don't listen. Sounds appalling.

## Welcome to Midulthood

.....................................................................................

# PERCENTAGES: WHAT ARE MIDULTS MADE OF?

- 10 per cent needing to pee. Is it because of all the coffee, tea, green juices and gallons of water we are drinking? Or is it because our vaginas are crying tiny tears?
- 5 per cent terrible thoughts. You know the ones. Like 'I wonder what he looks like naked?' or 'When will you just bloody go ahead and die?'
- 35 per cent stressed. What? Not 97 per cent stressed? Not 99 per cent stressed? No, a lot of the time we are actually very Zen, calm, meditative, get shit done kinda grown-ups. 65 per cent of the time it works every time.
- 21 per cent snaccidents (*see* page 63). Look at us so disciplined, so firm, so, 'No I couldn't possibly manage a pudding.' (It's because we already ate the fridge.)
- 47 per cent needing to sleep. Always need sleep. Would you like a private island? Only if I could sleep there. Wouldn't it be nice to just fall asleep when you hit the pillow and wake up 8 hours later? Rather than have to make 24 sacrifices to the gods and still wake up at 4.45am?
- 5 per cent wanting to buy something really inappropriate. Like glittery boots. Or leather leggings. When what you really need is a raincoat and a nice summer jumper. And some new knickers. *buys the leather*
- 27 per cent swear words. As in 'The washing machine is buggering about' and 'What kind of fucker doesn't thank you when you graciously give way in the car?' and 'What the cunting hell am I supposed to say to that?'
- 3 per cent dreaming of the moisturiser that is going to make you look like a sun-kissed 22-year-old.
- 2 per cent worrying about whether we should have paid more attention in maths: So that our finances wouldn't be such a mystery. And the rest.

## Chapter 9

# IN MY DEFENCE, I WAS LEFT UNSUPERVISED

BY THIS POINT IN THIS BOOK, you may think that we (by now you have probably realised that, by 'we', we mean 'you' too) are extremely hard to please. Apart from all the feelings, we can appear to be so complete. So self-reliant. So, 'Oh for God's sake I'll do it.' Low bullshit tolerance and high alert dickdar. Our aversion to disposable things and people. Our tendency to think in direct relation to our experience.

And yet we are almost uniquely easy to please. Tiny things make us happy. Simple pleasures can take us from disheartened to hopeful in a nanosecond. A compliment that is not generalised, but rather specific and sincere and spontaneous can make us feel seen and known and swishy in an instant. A waft of fabric conditioner on the t-shirt of someone we love. Odd little moments when the world seems to be taking care of us: it stops raining just as we walk out of the hairdresser; our bra doesn't hurt; we stumble upon the belief that good things are in the post. And by post, we mean both ASOS and karma. They are on their way. Perhaps, there's a joy-trigger so subtle that we can't even identify it, but it ignites a flash of sunshine in our soul. The sticky wicket is identifying the happiness amid the emotional white noise.

Does happiness feel like something that is meant for other people? Do you dare to be happy? Like all affairs of the heart, it's a risk. This is not to say that you don't laugh and love but perhaps you are a bit haunted by the...pretending. A bit dark side of the moon.

Because, now and again, when you stumble upon a pocket of joy, it feels almost mysterious. You think, 'I feel most peculiar. Am I coming down with something?' You pause for a moment and snuggle into the feeling, and wonder if this might be...happiness. Not mania or excitement or sheer speediness. Hmmm. Joy. Which is what happens when we let it.

So, if you've managed to slow down for long enough to recognise this situation, then what do you do? How can you trust this strange, trippy feeling of contentment that may have come from a flower or a sky or a smile or a parking space or a job or a kiss? How to rely on this fickle, fast-moving, fair-weather feeling?

Happiness is a sprite. Feelings are naughty. They run away. Thoughts, however, belong – at least a little – to you. So, we have found that, when we are blindsided by a slice of joy, it helps to just...notice. Just stop. And see how it feels. And, apparently, you will be chiselling a new neural pathway and forming a healthy little habit. Get to know it. Make it your friend. Whack out the welcome mat so that it might want to visit you more often. Leave a light on in the window. Not in a prostitute way.

# Porn Again

You know all about property porn (*see* page 80). You've probably got Zoopla open right now; it's your gateway to another world, another life. One with a 70ft garden, or a terrace overlooking the river or a second bathroom. Yes! Yes! Ye—

But what about all the other porn? The other delights we like to indulge in. Like...

### Crying Porn
Just going about my business ordering a Deliveroo and watching *Terms of Endearment*/ the one with Meryl Streep and Dustin Hoffman/the one where Julianne Moore gets Alzheimer's at 50 and crying and crying and crying. Howling. A great big cleansing wail...Oh God, so good.

### Podcast Porn
Look at all the podcasts I subscribe to. I am the queen of the podcasts. I am SO HOT for podcasts right now.

### Insta-Porn
There I am lying in bed with my thumb gently stroking...my iPhone screen as I deep dive into Instagram. A deep, deep, drill down. A never-ending, completely addictive, serotonin-reducing loop, exposing other people's curated lives. Nearly incredibly satisfying but...not. Edging. In a way.

### Cancel Porn
Cancel me, cancel me, cancel me harder.

### Holiday Porn
Where shall I go? Peru? Shall I detox? Or walk the Alps? Shall I go solo? Am I too young for a cruise? And once you've made a commitment, there's the hot and heavy foreplay – you probably keep the hotel/hostel/country open on your browser so you can have a quick hit of your hot holiday whenever you want. Thought: is booking actually the sexiest bit?

### Food Box Porn
I get Farmdrop, Abel & Cole, HelloFresh and the other one. You can't get through my front door without grazing your shins on my wonky vegetables and fresh eggs. There's nothing like a fresh delivery to get me excited about cooking again. What the fuck am I going to do with all these turnips? *sobs*

# Mini Mood Enhancers

One key to survival is accessing tiny pockets of joy. Not life-changing epiphanies or even healthy habits, but small stolen pleasures. Little plasters for the soul. Like…

- Using the posh cutlery. Yes it's just you, and yes you are just eating a takeaway. But sometimes a weighty fork gives you a lift. Hell, a linen napkin too, rather than recycled kitchen roll. Or your tracksuit bottoms.
- Opening a fresh five pack of knickers. Oh, the ecstasy of the box-fresh five pack.
- Putting on noise-cancelling headphones…Ah…the gift of silence.
- Things that come with chips. Without having to ask. 'Oh I didn't know this soup, salad, pie came with chips. No it's OK, you can leave them here.'
- Dropping your phone and seeing it bounce all the way down the stairs, as you watch in growing horror. Time may be in slo-mo but your brain is making a million terrible calculations. And then it lands and, somehow, everything is completely fine.
- Asking, 'Can anyone else hear the ringing or is it me?' And someone says, 'Yes – I can hear the ringing. It is the telly.' The relief is enormous. You don't have late onset tinnitus from all the long-ago clubbing. Or dementia.
- Going out and having a really fun, stimulating, relatively cheap dinner and still being in bed by 10pm.
- Hearing, 'I thought that was your natural colour.' So what if they're lying. At this point, you'll take it.
- Getting into an absurdly hot bath and thinking, 'Yes, I am going to stay here forever.' (Obviously after five minutes you are half-boiled and barely conscious.)
- Realising that you are only one coffee in. The world is your goddam oyster, all you can see is the open road and all the coffee shops along the way.
- Waking up to the fact that you genuinely give zero fucks. 'So how are you feeling about this meeting/dinner/appointment/argument?' asks one of your inner demons in Paxman-tone? 'Honestly Jeremy, I give zero fucks about it.'
- Smiling at strangers – terrifying for beginners and you properly have to fake it. But then it gets cosy. And you start seeing people rather than merely swerving them.
- Answering the phone with 'Yo'. Why is this so cheering? Perhaps because it's so tragic but we are too old to care.
- Turning off the tap while brushing our teeth and feeling that we are very slightly saving the world.
- Meandering around a haberdashery department, fingering thimbles and interfacing. Surely nothing bad can happen here…
- Wearing improbably lurid lipstick around the house, so that every time we catch sight of ourselves unexpectedly it is joyful in a six-year-old way.

# Are You Staying In-In?

We all know about Out-Out. Not to be mistaken for the domestic and wieldy 'out'. Out-Out is a whole different kettle of panic. It's an occasion. A night out that you need to psych yourself up for: buy a new dress, highlight it in the diary, maybe fresh make-up and a hair-do. All braced for a real grown-up hangover that lasts two days and the knowledge that you might get frisky and forgetful. You need both cash and a shame spiral allowance. For all the fun you are going to have. This now happens once a year.

And then there's In-In. A night alone organised with the kind of military precision that only a Midult can unleash. Again diarised. This is no accidental 'Oh I can watch a bit of *Harry Met Sally* on Netflix while I do my tax return' night in. This is no 'So-and-so cancelled so I can catch up on laundry, how relaxing' night in.

This is you. And only you. There is no unplanned external interference. The doorbell must not ring. To cancel a night of In-In would be to cancel your entire self. It cannot be undone.

It will involve getting out the secret slipper socks that you definitely don't own and will deny knowledge of until you die. A specific combination of food. Maybe chilli from the freezer (this has been weeks in the planning). Or a hummus and tortilla chips fest (because who cares about garlic breath?) and several of those Gü things that you haven't bought for years because of the ramekin overload.

There will be a terrible TV series. Netflix will do that thing when it asks you if you are still watching. And you will stay up late. Recklessly late. 'Who even are you?' late?

You are hunkering down with yourself. You are in mini-retreat. You are saving your own life. You are In-In.

The laws of In-In:

1.  The first rule of In-In is tell no one. You will feel a bit shifty. Bliss.
2.  The second rule of In-In is you are not going to share it. With anyone. Even someone in crisis – and, yes, this does make you a terrible person but your In-In cannot be compromised.
3.  Phone off. No emails. Total cut-off.
4.  It starts and ends with a bath.
5.  Your entire fridge must be a snaccident waiting to happen. Load it up, people.

# Tiny Petty Victories

Most of the time we try to be nice. We do. The intention is there. But what about when we are feeling a bit like Sisyphus, every day pushing up a rock that is obviously going to roll down again, or sprout little baby rocks or hairs or laundry? Well, there are times when pettiness, like swearing, helps. There are pointless little victories to be had out there. A bit mean-spirited perhaps, but no one is going to die. Probably no one is even going to notice. And winning is winning.

## I Want The Banquette
You have the banquette it's OK. I am not sure whether the chair or the banquette is better for my back anyway. I mean probably the banquette but...And the thing is, I'm a bit claustrophobic. No it's OK you have the banquette. OK I'll have the banquette.

## I Am In Control
I'VE GOT THE REMOTE. NAH NAH NAH NAH NAH (sung internally).

## I Can't See You
When you pretend not to see someone frantically trying to change lane because they are stuck behind a bus or some scaffolders or who cares? Just not sorry.

## I Am Faster
Also when someone overtakes you and you overtake them ten minutes later. Take that motherfucker. You *may* have said that out loud.

## I Am Not Cancelling
You both want to cancel. It's a game of chicken like that scene in *Footloose* with the tractors and Kevin Bacon's foot gets stuck in the pedals. Anyway you hold out, you hold out and BOOM they are the one who cancels. You get a night in and the moral high ground. Plus a cancel in the bank. Is there anything better than a cancel in the bank? It's two nights in. Not that we are counting.

## I'm Hanging Up First
Person: Goodb— Oh.

## I Am First
New queue, new queue, and even though you were way, way back you get to the front. You are internally punching the air. And everyone hates you. But you hate everyone back, so that's OK.

## I Am Right
When you are right about something. Like a bad boyfriend or a cheap shoe or both. And you are not going to say, 'I told you so'. And you are not going to say, 'I'm not going

to say it', which is infinitely worse. Instead you give the look. Because you told them so. And you are not going to say it.

**I Am Not Going Anywhere**
You know when someone wants to get rid of you and they are busy washing up, and getting their clothes ready for tomorrow and taking the bins out, but you ask for a herbal tea? And the herbal tea is hotter than hell and everyone is in for another 45 minutes. Why do you do this? What is wrong with you?

**I Am Soooo Relaxed**
Look at me leaving the fridge door open until it beeps. Look at you all twitchy and unable to handle the idea that all that precious coldness is flooding out into the room. What a shame that you are so tense. Poor you.

# I Am Having A Ball

I'm waiting to feel defeated. That day will come. But, as things stand, as I live and breathe, I am having a ball. I am eating everything that isn't nailed down. Yes, I'm probably expanding gently but – never having been a painted-on-clothes kind of person – I have some wriggle room in my jeans. Less and less. But it doesn't feel drastic. I'm not in the mood for drastic.

And I am smoking. In the garden. In the rain. In the morning with a cup of coffee before anyone else wakes up. Feeling faintly fuck you but also vaguely chesty. And when you smoke, you want to drink. So I'm doing that too. Not a civilised glass of red wine but an even more civilised bottle. Not twice a week but five times. Not including cocktails. The eating helps with the hangovers.

And I'm shopping. Christmas shopping for myself. I keep seeing things I fancy – which never happens – so I am buying them. It's Zara not YSL but still, the back door is falling off and I need a root canal. Instead I choose to buy some pretty things. To drink in and eat in and shop in.

I'm a grown-up. I know that this is not sustainable. Not if I want to stay who I am and remain in my life. And I like my life. It's just that at the moment I am particularly ENJOYING my life. Just diving into the frippery fun. It's not meditation. It's not yoga. It's not supplements and sleep hygiene and long-term self-care. No, I am having a bit of a holiday. In my life.

# Conversations You Have With Yourself In The Bath

Me:        Nice.
Also me:   Too hot.
Me:        Don't have to talk to anyone.
Also me:   Why didn't I bring my phone in here? What if someone is trying to get hold of me?
Me:        I can totally switch off.
Also me:   They might think I slipped and banged my head and am now unconscious and possibly dead.
Me:        I'm going to let myself not worry for 20 minutes.
Also me:   I feel like I might die soon.
Me:        Just going to calmly and meticulously shave my legs.
Also me:   I may cut myself and bleed to death.
Me:        I'm enjoying this Radio 4 Extra play about the Romanovs.
Also me:   Who all died before their time like I will.
Me:        Feeling quite sleepy.
Also me:   Like Whitney Houston just before she drowned.
Me:        Must get a pedicure and a wax this week.
Also me:   Don't want anyone judging me when they find my corpse.
Me:        This expensive conditioning bath oil my sister gave me is so nice.
Also me:   She thinks I need it because my skin is so withered.
Me:        Bit slippy in here. Did I use too much? Will I have to clean the bath as soon as I get out?
Also me:   Your mindless extravagance is why you will die penniless.
Me:        But it makes me feel rich and spoilt – like Marie Antoinette.
Also me:   She was decapitated of course.
Me:        Or Cleopatra.
Also me:   Suicide.
Me:        Might do a facemask.
Also me:   Can't be arsed to do a facemask.
Me:        Where's the one that makes me look 25?
Also me:   In your dreams.
Me:        I am getting really good at this beauty stuff.
Also me:   Maybe learn to take your make-up off properly before you get too smug. You look like a panda. An old one.

## Chapter 10

# I AM DYNAMIC, I AM INVINCIBLE, I AM EXHAUSTED

ARE YOU TIRED ALL THE TIME? As tired in the morning as you are at night? As knackered after a big sleep as after a bad, bad night? Have you permanently got an autumn in your step despite dragging yourself to HIIT training twice a week and giving up wheat? Have you had your thyroid, hormones, iron and everything else tested and it all looks normal: you rattle with supplements but you feel like the living dead; existing in a twilight world where your eyes feel a bit stingy and your limbs feel a bit leaden and you regularly bounce off walls like a drunk person even though you're too scared to get drunk because you are so tired? Are you tired after holidays and tired after weekends?

Tiredness isolates. You do less, see less, talk less. You are at capacity with earning enough money to live and keeping any family relationships alive so you are very much not the funnest girl at the party. In fact, if you even made it to the party, you probably left before it even got fun.

If you are one of those turbo-charged types then you are blessed beyond words and should turn the page. Because this chapter is about recognition that many of us are so exhausted. How many times have you thought 'I am so tired' today? Did you wake up thinking, 'I am so tired'? Did you spend ten minutes sitting on the side of the bed, wrapped in a towel staring at the wall, thinking, 'How am I going to manage?' Did you think, 'If I just get through today and then get to bed by 9pm then maybe I will make it through tomorrow'?

We talk more about sleep than we do about sex. If your tiredness is down to insomnia then the likelihood is, you not only feel tired, you feel poisoned. Filled with dread. You begin to doubt yourself, and you lose your jaunt, your joy, your frisk; you feel like a dried-up husk that no amount of facial oil can slick. You are held together with concealer and dry shampoo and hundreds of coffees. You see blurry shapes out of the corners of your eyes and when you whip your head round to capture them, they vanish. You hear colours. And all the while you are pretending that you are a fully operational human woman. Because tiredness is so dull, right?

Occasionally, terrifyingly, you manage to flip it so that you are tired-not-tired. You are high on tiredness. You are on fire. You are a ninja. You are making extremely good – although unlikely – decisions. You buy a frilly denim jacket online (what's not to like about frilly denim when you are over 40?) while transferring money to a plumber while booking a flight (no, you don't need to concentrate on one thing because you are on

FIRE) while also driving. Not really. Maybe. Ssshhhh. No surrender. Because you are so over being tired. So overtired…oh.

To be so tired that you no longer feel tired is to exist in an altered state – suspended between rapture and despair. You become a kind of high-pitched squeak hanging in the universe. Human white noise. 'I don't need sleep,' you think. 'I've got this covered.' Three words: go to bed.

But that's perverse, because bed is now the enemy, however clean the pillows, high the thread count and ironed the sheets. You are desperate to get back there, and yet, oh look there it is again, another flavour of dread: bed dread. Because you know that your brain is gearing up to wake you at 3am to screen a medley of your most humiliating moments.

And while we are here, staring at the damp corner in the ceiling that we can't afford to fix right now, let's not forget the weird kind of wakefulness that means you can write the headlines for your brilliant strategy report, or the first chapter of your novel or a brilliant riposte to the arsehole email you read just before you turned the light off. None of which you will remember in the morning. Night vision amplifies and then deletes.

You fall asleep everywhere and not in the fun way you used to when you were in your twenties: under your desk at work because you had been up drinking cheap wine until three; on an Indian train with just a sarong, a backpack and a ratty Jackie Collins paperback for company. Now you wake up on the sofa at 11.13pm and it's cold – there may be dribble and the rustle of a crisp packet, and you know you've fucked it. And the cycle begins again.

Maybe, in the absence of sleep or restedness, we just have to accept that being a grown-up is being tired all the time: you tell people you feel tired and they tell you how tired they are back. God, I am tired today. How did you sleep?

## I'm More Tired Than You

Me: I'm so tired.
You: Me too.
Me: Like, REALLY exhausted.
You: Shattered beyond the point of madness.
Me: I'm just not sleeping.
You: I haven't slept in – well, I can't remember how long.
Me: Yes, my short-term memory has been affected by no sleep too.
You: What were we even talking about?
Me: I can't remember, I'm too tired.
You: You're quite hard to understand, you know.
Me: Am I talking like a demonic record being played backwards?

You: …………

Me: Hello?

You: Sorry, I just had a micro-sleep.

Me: I wish I could have a micro-sleep.

You: Six seconds is the longest I have slept in about a year.

Me: Only a year! You're so lucky.

You: Probably two years, actually, don't forget the memory loss.

Me: Six seconds is like a lie-in for me.

You: I've tried everything – sleeping pills—

Me: Not even recreationally fun, they're so ineffective.

You: Sleep CDs—

Me: I mean, stop talking, I'm trying to sleep!

You: Positive affirmations—

Me: 'I allow my raging evil brain of death to switch off and let go.'

You: Melatonin—

Me: For amateurs and children.

You: Hypnosis—

Me: You lost me at, 'You are feeling very sleepy.'

You: I've basically been awake for most of my adult life.

Me: I feel like I've been awake since Robbie Williams was still with Take That.

You: I feel like I've been awake since before I was born.

Me: Since before my parents met.

You: When dinosaurs roamed the Earth.

Me: Sometimes I feel so tired I just want to kill myself.

You: I'm too tired to kill myself, I just can't be arsed.

Me: I don't have the energy to even argue with you.

You: Brain. Melting. Won't. Form. Sentences.

Me: Help.

You: Can't, too tired.

## 48 Things You've Done Before 8am

Early morning is a remarkably fertile time of doing many, many things really quite badly. Or, if not badly, then incompletely. Like:

1. Ordered online delivery – yes, I am dynamic, I am invisible. Sorry, invincible.
2. Decided to go to the theatre.
3. Decided the theatre is a stupid idea.

4. Put a white wash on. Then cancelled it because left a trail of socks on the stairs. Put it on again. Find a t-shirt in the corridor. Howl.
5. Googled house prices. Got distracted by sex scandal. Texted friend about sex scandal.
6. Thought about checking bank balance. Too early for depressing news though.
7. Tried to find the paper bit of your driver's licence.
8. Opened laptop while eating porridge.
9. Dripped the maple syrup on keyboard.
10. Called the maple syrup a fucker.
11. Wondered if it was OK to have a fourth coffee.
12. Wrote a list for the shrink: boundaries, bad back, dead dad.
13. Drank Berocca. Can't afford to get ill.
14. Took womany vitamins. Can't afford to be womany.
15. Googled natural anti-anxiety supplements.
16. Took vitamin B for…what's vitamin B for again?
17. Emailed accountant about tax return.
18. Googled 'What is a pension?'
19. Debated whether or not to cancel plans tonight. Desperate to. Whose turn is it to cancel? Yours or theirs?
20. Stared at phone for a bit.
21. Set up a WhatsApp family group.
22. Regretted instantly.
23. Shaved legs sitting in the bath while listening to five minutes of a podcast about American politics. Feel like an authority.
24. Stubbed toe on door frame. Called door frame a bastard.
25. Cried a little.
26. Took ibuprofen for back/period/head/knee/soul pain.
27. Decided to get new haircut.
28. Changed mind about haircut.
29. Fifth coffee?
30. Wondered about Ritalin. Everyone seems to be stealing it from teenagers.
31. Wondered if there was time to go back to bed for ten minutes.
32. Listened to the *Today* programme for three minutes. Am now fully informed and armed for conversation.
33. Took mind off anxiety by spending five minutes on Lakeland.co.uk salivating over hangers with clips on.
34. Made plan to upgrade hangers. Will def do that. So going to do that.
35. Stared at wardrobe hoping for something stylish and flattering to leap out.

36. Phone was buzzing. Searched for phone. Where the fuck is…?
37. Found phone. Answered breathlessly. PPI call.
38. Threw phone.
39. Tried to locate nearest Hermes parcel drop for all the second-hand designer clothes you are going to sell for huge amounts of money.
40. Cancelled plans.
41. Sat on bed for ten minutes in a towel. Feeling tired. And then cold.
42. Wondered about whether or not to buy a dressing gown. Would you wear a dressing gown?
43. Checked bank balance.
44. Decided against dressing gown.
45. Sucked on a vape until ears bled.
46. Liked every post on Instagram so no one will know you might be depressed.
47. Went into bathroom and stared at the changing face of you for what felt like a long, long time.
48. Discussed how much sleep you got with your best friend, work wife, the dog, the stranger on the overground and the Starbucks person (Me: It's only the fifth coffee, I'm absolutely fine. Narrator: Everything was not absolutely fine.)

## Adventures In Insomnia: When Your Brain Turns Nasty

INT. A suburban bedroom.

Deep, dark night. A ravishingly vital and not remotely sweaty woman is in bed. We close in on the corner of her fitted sheet, which has pinged off. Cue brain.

Brain: Whoa. I've just realised something terrible.

You:  No, no, no. I'm asleep…What?

Brain: You're so OLD.

You:  You woke me up to say that?

Brain: Just think about that for a second. All the things you HAVEN'T done.

You:  I'm going to try not to, actually, because it's 3.30am, you absolute psycho.

Brain: You don't own this house, for example.

You:  Most of Europe rents…

Brain: Not exactly married, are you?

You:  What is this, the Fifties? Shut up, I'm trying to sleep.

Brain: No money.

You:  I have money.

Brain: No, you don't.

You:  Compared to some people, I do.

Brain: Haven't done your tax return yet though, have you? Because you're scared.
You:   I'm only a bit scared.
Brain: You're so BROKE.
You:   My therapist says I am rich in other ways.
Brain: OMG, you fool.
You:   Takes one to know one. You're meant to be on my side.
Brain: You need to face these things.
You:   No I don't, it's THE MIDDLE OF THE ACTUAL NIGHT.
Brain: You might die soon, you know.
You:   Given this current conversation, that might actually be welcome.
Brain: Alone. Penniless. With a beard...
You:   I do NOT have a beard.
Brain: Yet.
\*REPEATS FOR THE NEXT FOUR HOURS\*

# All The Sleep Cures We've Tried

Perky? Or tired? Big tired? Or little tired? We cannot assume anything about your relationship with sleep but, really, who sleeps? Here are just a few of the things we have tried so far this year to help. With sleep. Or lack thereof. Sleep. One word. Such power. Here are just a few of the things we have tried so far this year to help us sleep. Sorry are we repeating ourselves?

### Night-Time Yoga
This was in itself an act of desperation seeing as we have been swerving the namaste for years. But there is a relatively non-annoying YouTuber called Adriene from Austin, Texas, whose classes are both free and tolerable. So, wholeheartedly, we tried one. And fell asleep at 11pm until 2am. So that was that. Smell ya later, Adriene.

### Lavender
Fuck off.

### A Continental Sleep Clinic
Off we went in good faith. A discreet tablet was slid under our mattress to measure the old REM. It showed, the next morning, that we had slept for one hour and 57 minutes. 'You are going to have a heart attack!!!!!!!!' barked the sleep counsellor the following morning. 'You need medical help!!!!!!!' I thought that's why I was here. 'This programme is not for you!!!!!!!!!' So why did we carve out three days and get on a plane

to come here? We left early and arrived home utterly deranged and basically broken. Too splintered to even get cross. The dreary yet inevitable 'tell us about your experience' email landed. 'Ummm…maybe don't market whatever that was as a sleep programme.'

### Positive Mental Attitude

'I am a brilliant sleeper. I sleep beautifully, fully, completely. The night gives me everything I need. I will never have trouble sleeping again. I will wake up rested, refreshed and ready for my day. I have an actual talent when it comes to sleep. I am gifted with regard to sleep.' How do you think that went?

### Brandy And A Biscuit

Lovely drift off and then a parched/sugar-low-sit-bolt-upright moment at 3am and the rest of the night to luxuriate in death fantasies while fingering a chin hair.

### Cough And Cold Mixture

The sleep of the dead. Followed by the hangover of the mighty. Except we are clearly not mighty. Driving, talking, thinking pretty much impossible for 48 hours. We call it the Green Honey: the nectar of the devil.

### Meditation

Is this man's voice sexy or sinister? Did we defrost the chicken? Clear the mind, clear the mind, clear the mind. Woke up at 3am with headphones tourniqueted around neck. That's relaxing.

### Sleep Hygiene

No screens. No telly. No laptop. No phone. No Kindle. No iPad. No sleep. Also going to bed at same time every night and waking up at same time too. Vigilant about this. So bed at 11. And up at 3. Marv.

### Hypnosis

We were definitely hypnotised in that chair. We remember nothing so it must have worked. We are feeling quietly confident. We can feel that our brain has been somehow rewired. It's a miracle. We are cured. That shimmering, twilight, heart-poundy, adrenaline-charged chapter of our life is over. Glory be. We tuck ourselves in and drift off. Until 3am.

### Hormones

Aha. We are in our early forties. The beginning of the sleepless years. We shall conquer our hormones and we shall prevail. We shall turn the perimenopausal years into a power surge. The hormones do help with the anxiety and our hair seems thicker and our attitude is powerful. And we sleep through until? Guess…Yup. Again.

### Cutting Out Coffee

Because the acupuncturist says it does evil things to our liver. That we will see and feel the difference when we eliminate this demon from our life. Our systems will entirely realign and all will be well and we shall sleep the sleep of the virtuous and the blessed. Tried it. For a week. Now pass the triple shot capp and shut up. Please. Begging.

### Not Drinking Water After 6pm

Because, well, bladders. Bladders that we have clearly established are the size of bath pearls – remember those? So we wake parched at 3am and reach for the water, knock it over onto (or, more accurately, into) our laptop. That cunning little plan just cost us a thousand quid. Surely that's worth a few more sleepless nights…

## Don't Tell Me I Look Tired

Let's get one thing straight. Telling someone they look tired is telling someone they look awful. It's not helpful. Stop saying it. 'Aw, you look tired,' with a head tilt, creased brow and protruding lower lip. Now this might be intended to be supportive; the act of a sympathetic person who is concerned about your mental health/sleeping habits. But let's not be cute about this. It's just someone telling you you look like hell. Nobody looks good when they are tired. Nobody feels good when they are tired. Why is this being remarked upon? Not constructive.

Telling someone they look exhausted is a bit more sympathetic. More gracious, somehow. More romantic. Less an implication that someone looks bloody awful and more a sweeping observation about their general (tragic) aura. No puffy eyes and wan complexion specificity. A person knows when they are tired, OK? The last thing they need is you pointing it out to them. It's there for the whole world to see, written all over their face like a dreary sign. If you are dealing with a tired person, hold back. They will not be feeling perky and cheerful and in the mood for some gentle ribbing. That's fine for hangovers – people expect to be told they look like shit. It's practically a badge of honour. But tired people don't have the energy for a commentary, however accurate it may be. They're tired. And they look terrible. Do them a favour and talk about something else. Or be honest and just tell them they look terrible. At least then everyone will know where they stand.

# Seize Every Napportunity

Obviously if we find a window, we fill it with a nap. But not all naps are equal. They come in a dizzying variety of flavours.

### The Refresher Nap

This is the alpha of the nap family. The ulti-nap. It's a 30-minute wonder that actually leaves you feeling refreshed rather than drunk. You don't weave out of the bedroom and bump into the coffee table. It's the nap that leaves your face looking peachy-fresh rather than imprinted with pillow-lines. You think, 'I actually woke up like this!' as you shake your hair girlishly in the mirror. (This nap is a rarity. Never give up hope though.)

### The Sofa Nap

You've managed to find a use for your grocery box vegetables and cooked some kind of casserole thing that was almost delicious. Strangely you are watching something in real-time, having temporarily exhausted all your box set options. You are on the sofa and neither quite awake not quite asleep but certainly chilly.

### The Out-Out Nap

Yes you are Out-Out tonight. You are going to stay up past ten. Past midnight even. So you need to bank some hours, sacrifice a bit of daylight to those capricious sleep gods. (Obvs you know that that doesn't work but who can risk the ire?) 'Clear my afternoon people I am having a power nap,' you say to no one in particular. Also known as a disco nap.

### The Siesta

The one where it would be rude not to because you are on holiday and you have to respect local culture. This may be reason enough to move to Spain.

### The I've Been Hit By A Brick Nap

You are eating the soup/having the chat/doing the admin when you suddenly realise you have no option but to lie down, on top of the bed with all your clothes on and your jewellery. The last thing you think before you pass out is, 'Shit, I've got my contacts in.'

### The Hangover Nap

Oof the relief of slipping into cool sheets when you've got a raging hot hangover. Yes everything is spinning; yes, you will feel worse not better when you wake up and will have to eat your bodyweight in pizza. But right now it's just you and the cool sheets. Except why can't you sleep? The wakefulness is a kind of penance...

# Adventures In Insomnia: The Damp Patch

INT. A suburban bedroom.

Deep, dark night. A remarkably unlined woman is in bed, muttering to herself. The camera pans towards an ominous-looking shadow – could it be her soul? – on the ceiling. Cue brain.

Brain: That damp patch on the ceiling.

Me: I know, don't bring it up.

Brain: What if it's still leaking?

Me: It's not, the flat upstairs turned their water off. Stop talking.

Brain: What if they lied?

Me: They didn't lie. I'm trying to sleep.

Brain: You should check the damp patch in case the ceiling is about to fall in.

Me: It's 3am. I don't need to check it, I need to sleep.

Brain: You should check it.

Me: No.

Brain: Check it.

Me: Aargh!

Brain: CheckCheckCheckCheck.

(gets up, checks, comes back to bed)

Brain: It looked bigger to me.

Me: It wasn't bigger.

Brain: Yeah, it was bigger.

Me: I just checked it. You were there. We both saw it. It's not bigger.

Brain: ............'kay.

Me: Christ, is it bigger?

Brain: Don't ask me, what do I know? You're the expert.

(gets up again, checks it, comes back to bed)

Me: Well, now I can't tell if it's bigger.

Brain: Dangerous...

Me: Maybe I should move the sofa. It's right underneath it. What if it gets damaged?

Brain: Maybe you should move out.

Me: What?

Brain: This isn't even your house. You're just renting because you don't have enough money to look after yourself and buy your own house because you are a failure who doesn't earn enough.

Me: Whoa.

Brain: SPICEGIRLSSONGSPICEGIRLSSONGSPICEGIRLSSONG.
Me: Don't give this horror story a soundtrack!!!
Brain: 'STOPRIGHTNOW.'
Me: No, YOU stop right now, brain of Satan.
Brain: You started it.
Me: I hate you.
Brain: MORNING!

## Bedtime Busy-Ness

Bedtime does not necessarily go in a straight line. The moment you slide between the sheets something strikes you as unavoidably urgent and you feel compelled to...

1. Realise that you haven't washed your hair for three days. Is that too long? You have a meeting at 8.30am. Plus you've run out of dry shampoo.
2. Go to put dry shampoo on the grocery order. Realise you've left your phone in the other room as part of a sleep hygiene programme that isn't working. You've missed the deadline for the order. Put a reminder on your phone to buy dry shampoo on way to work.
3. Lay out work outfit. Might as well. You are now ahead of self. High five.
4. Check for stains on shirt. Sniff shirt's armpits. Hmmm.
5. Put phone back in other room. It needs to be charged. But charger is by bed from before you started the sleep hygiene programme. Go get charger.
6. Should you order another charger? How many chargers is too many chargers?
7. Go for just-in-case pee.
8. Is everything off/locked?
9. Go round home death-proofing everything. Still feel residual death/burglar paranoia.
10. Hang up towels. Sniff towels. Sniff flannel. Sniff self. Feel slight sense of shame.
11. Do 20 seconds of pelvic floor exercises.
12. Shit! Eye cream!
13. While you are in the bathroom, apply some fake tan. Might as well.
14. Also need to check breasts. Get phone to Google how to check breasts.
15. Back into bed. Accidentally rub heel against other foot. Nearly lacerate self as it's been *a while* since a pedicure. Find some foot cream and socks. Apply.
16. Go for just-in-case pee.
17. Worry about fake tan on pillow for a bit. Try to fall asleep on back.
18. But did you blow out that candle?

# Adventures In Insomnia: What Does This Pain Mean?

INT. A suburban bedroom.

Deep, dark night. A remarkably young-looking woman is in bed. Her foot – pedicured, but bunioned – has escaped the duvet and is twitching. Cue brain.

Brain: It's probably just a bruise.

Me: (waking up) Whaaa?

Brain: That pain in your toe.

Me: Can we not? I was dreaming about Michael Hutchence.

Brain: Look, I don't want to be – no, doesn't matter.

Me: What?

Brain: Nothing, forget I said anything.

Me: No, go on.

Brain: You don't think it could be…(whispers) something worse?

Me: I kicked a ball. That's all. It's nothing.

Brain: We don't know anything at this stage.

Me: This is ridiculous, I'm going back to sleep.

Brain: Bob Marley kicked a football and it gave him cancer.

Me: It did not give him cancer, the cancer was already there.

Brain: So what you're saying is, kicking the football alerted him to the cancer.

Me: Yes.

Brain: Because it made his toe painful.

Me: Yes.

Brain: …………

Me: Oh.

Brain: They'll probably have to amputate. You might lose a foot.

Me: Oh, COME ON.

Brain: It's probably better if they take your whole leg, actually. Safer.

Me: OMG.

Brain: They could just chop you in half and save your torso. At least you'll still be able to do your hair and make-up.

Me: Wait, I—

Brain: Unless it's already too late…

Me: Too late?

Brain: I'd go for a Viking Burial.

Me: How did we—

Brain: You could be on a boat and someone really handsome could fire a flaming arrow into it.

Me:  I want singing too.

Brain: Maybe a Welsh choir or a solitary chorister…

Me:  (tearful)

Brain: Everyone clutching each other's hands, crying.

Me:  Telling stories about me…

Brain: …The flaming boat with your body on board getting stuck in the reeds as your husband starts eyeing up your sister in her hot black bodycon dress.

Me:  Hang on, she doesn't wear things like that.

Brain: She lost a lot of weight. Because of the stress of you dying.

Me:  I don't believe this.

Brain: It's probably just a bruise.

## Welcome to Midulthood

# LIES
# WE TELL
# EVERY DAY

### Can't Wait To See You
Sometimes this is true. Most times it just isn't. But it's not personal. I am just a bit tired.

### Everything's Going Brilliantly. I Am Really Excited About How It's All Going
I am terrified.

### Oh, No Thanks, I Am Full
(She was never full.)

### Of Course I Was Listening
I was. Took it all in. Every last word. Yup. What?

### You Are Right
You are not right. But I just need you to stop talking. So if agreeing with you is what needs to happen in order to make that happen, then I guess you are right.

### I Am Sorry
I say I am sorry all the time. But am I really sorry? Like really, really sorry? Genuinely repentant and regretful? Probably not. Sorry.

### No Worries
I say 'no worries' a helluva lot for someone who is exploding with worry.

### No I'm Not On Instagram While You Are Talking
*stares into the Midult distance*

### I Didn't Hear My Phone
(Because it was on silent.)

### I Hope You Are Well
I write this on all my emails. I hope you are well, person I have never met. Obviously I do not wish you ill but I don't really know if I have enough in the care bank to really mind about your health or wellness. And starting emails is always a bit awkward, if I am honest. Which it is clear that I am not.

### I Do Not Want To Know…
…that piece of gossip you haven't finished telling me, the latest WhatsApp group, what the weather is going to be like, how much 'money' is in my bank account. Except I do.

# Chapter 11

# WISHBONE, BACKBONE, FUNNY BONE

YOU KNOW WHO YOU ARE. We are planning our silver friend-i-versary party. They mock us for our starry-eyedness: 'Perhaps you should express your love for each other through the medium of interpretive dance?' Perhaps. With ribbons on sticks and a Richard Clayderman soundtrack. That would be an eye-opener.

We vividly remember the moment we met. You, struck by my busty theatricality. I, dazed in the face of your tawnily shy charisma. Both of us knowing that this would be more than a one-night thing. The universe squishing us together in the age of innocence and then beating the hell out of us over the years so that, sometimes, we could only surface, gasp for air, look each other in the eye and then keep going.

We were soon an acknowledged couple. Far from exclusive – if jealousy had been a problem we would never have lasted this long – but everyone knew that we were each other's chosen one.

We threw ourselves into threesomes, foursomes, orgies of conversation and exploration. We were non-negotiable. We've never said 'best friend'. Except maybe drunk or on Christmas Day or behind each other's backs. But we do say 'chosen family'. I am your most successful relationship and you are the love of my life.

The world in which we live, the one where family has become fractured, strange-shaped and fluid, where women are no longer passed from father to husband and expected to find all their emotional sustenance from their children, the one where a marriage is not for life, perhaps not even for Christmas; in this world, we have made our friends our family.

There are bumps and crunches, obviously. Female friendship is not uncomplicated (beautiful things rarely are). It begins so very intensely, when we are girls, trying out life and often getting it wrong. There is the manipulation, the jealousy, the bitchiness, the neediness, the spectacular fallings out, sharing beds, clothes, everything. Boys, with their football, acne and gentle buffoonery, can only watch in confusion and mounting terror. But as we grow, the fierceness of those early friendships, with their heartbreaking fall-outs and power plays, tames into a sort of bone-deep nurture.

Friendship is the delicious discovery of connection, shared thinking: a vibrational frequency that feels familiar, and forms a barrier against loneliness. It recognises that we are more alike than we are different. It is not a genetic thing, which is why siblings don't always work; you need to find your friends, and they have to find you. But that moment of discovery is one of the most thrilling experiences life has to offer. The beginning of a lifelong trip.

We all get things wrong, only pretend people are perfect. Sometimes forgiveness is required. Trails will fork and we might find ourselves in different places to the people we love the most. One might be feeling fractured and insane just as the other has found some sort of untouchable human nirvana with life, love, work and linen cupboard all in perfect harmony. Belief systems clash: one might actually find God while the other is still certain that immortality is for idiots. One is Leave, the other is Remain, one marches for women, the other wonders what all the fuss is about...Sometimes you find that you have travelled too far along different paths and don't know each other any more, and then it might be time to let go, gently. But most often we find a way back to each other. More and more women are quietly planning to pool resources and grow old together. Isn't that a relaxing thought? We share a loyalty that has become a talisman of hope.

But, back to you. From where I'm standing it's looking like till death do us part. So crank up the Richard Clayderman and fetch my leotard. I'm game if you are. I'm always game if you are.

## 11 Signs Someone Is A Good Friend

1. When you don't answer your phone because you're feeling sad and they text you and say, 'I know you're not answering your phone because you're feeling sad.'
2. They pick you up in their car so you don't have to do the walk of shame. Any kind of shame.
3. You can share a bed with them without it being awkward/weird.
4. You swap spare keys – even though you don't live that near to each other.
5. You're crying and they call you a 'total ****' just to make you laugh.
6. They quite happily pee in front of you. And vice versa.
7. They help you pack up/unpack when you move house – the most boring, stressful job that usually only family members find themselves roped into.
8. When telling them that your husband/partner/anyone doesn't ever seem to want to have sex with you makes you feel less ashamed.
9. When things are really terribly bad for you, they pop into your bedroom and make your bed. You don't notice until later.
10. They mind when you don't turn up. But only because they like the world better with you in sight.
11. They tell you your husband's on Tinder – no one else would.

## Why I Don't Fight With My Friends

There are two things you need from the people in your life, from the close people, the non-negotiable people, your people. And those two things are honesty and loyalty. This is why I do not get angry with my friends. Never. Because if they have my back then anything and everything that they do is OK.

We all slip up. We can get a bit overwhelmed and neglectful, a bit tired and crabby, a bit preoccupied and self-obsessed, a bit flaky and absent. Those things happen as energy and luck and happiness ebb and flow; as the contractions of panic and grief come and go. We are, none of us, perfect. And who wants brittle, shimmering perfection anyway? Give me the human beings not the cardboard cut-outs. Give me fallen man and woman with all their frailties and intricacies and glory.

Each of my dearest ones is slightly my mother and slightly my child. Comforting and to be cherished. It is heart-warming to see them fly and flourish, bruising to see them struggle. They can honestly do no wrong. Because – conversely in these deeply personal relationships – I feel free enough to take nothing personally.

Even in the closest friendships space is needed. Space to fuck things up now and again. Because when you give people room to grow, that's when you get the best of them. That's when everybody wins.

## How To Know If Your Friends Hate Your New Bloke

1. He is always referred to as your 'current boyfriend'.
2. They get his name wrong: 'How's David? I mean, Daniel, Danny, Dan. No, Dominic?'
3. They talk about your ex in front of him. 'I miss John.' 'If you had to say who the love of your life was, would you say John?' 'Remember when John said that thing??????' 'John would know how to fix that.' 'John was so handsome, it was sometimes hard to look at him.' 'Remember how everyone was in love with John!' 'Let's do a group selfie and send it to John.'
4. They never invite him to anything and then, when you arrive together, say, 'Oh!' in a surprised voice.
5. Friend: 'Did you watch *EastEnders* last night?' You: 'No, Damian was out last night and he wants to watch it together.' Friend: 'Unbelievable. So selfish…It's OK, you weren't to know he was totally wrong for you. When are you going to tell him it's over?'
6. They keep setting you up on blind dates. In front of him. 'My friend James from work is not only handsome, he's literally the funniest person I've ever met and he's

SUCH a good dancer. You should, like, marry him.' 'What are you doing next Tuesday? Do you want to have dinner with my brother? He's basically in love with you and you and you know your mother adores him and your father respects him.'

7. When you talk about him, they start sentences with, 'Look, I'll only say this once and then we can draw a line under it, but...'

8. They keep asking you if you're happy 'because you don't seem yourself' when you have just been saying how happy you are.

9. They keep referring to some mystery person called The Arsehole.

10. If they bump into you with your mother or sister they all share a sympathy look, like 'I know, we are all suffering'.

## Why Answering The Phone Is An Act Of Love

If you call me and I answer the phone, it means one of two things. Either you are a plumber and I am DESPERATE for you to help me. Or I really, really like you. Like, really like you. Because who calls anyone? And who picks up?

So. If the phone rings and someone answers, feel happy. Feel honoured. That's the first thing to know – your call has been answered where most would have been dropped. Absorb that compliment.

And then please don't get all entitled and sulky if someone answers only to say that they can't talk. They still answered. They didn't hit decline. They didn't do that awful, convenient, here's-one-I-made-earlier pre-packaged text thing of 'Sorry I can't talk right now', which makes everyone feel like chopped liver. They answered the phone, which means that – in the middle of a hectic life – they can *deal* with your voice. They can *face* the prospect of you.

And know this: if you get demanding about phone time and cross when someone has to go or it slips their mind to call you back then, slowly but certainly, the phone will no longer be answered. You will ooze into terrorist friend territory where handling the guilt of not talking to you is easier than handling you.

If you call me and I answer the phone, that is a declaration of love. And, for now, in the rush hour of everything, please let that be enough.

## Terrorist Friends

They are not enemies, apparently, but they are covertly acting to destroy us. Perhaps it is low self-esteem that makes them so desperate to assert their supremacy over us, so focused on holding all the power. But we are not here to explain or rationalise – that is the beginning of forgiveness. And we did too much of that. No, we are here to help you identify and excise your terrorist friends. We have been in the field, we are battle-scarred and wary. We have operational knowledge, we survived.

I saw her on the first day of secondary school. She radiated cool and I knew I had to make her my friend. It worked, we pricked our thumbs with a compass point and pressed them together so our blood would mingle. We had our first cigarette together, worked out a routine to 'Dancing Queen', our movements mirroring each other. Our friendship was intense, inviolate, envied, corrosive. She told me that the thing that was wrong with my face was my chin, she never let me forget that she was rich and I was poor, that she was thin and I was not, that she got boys and I did not. She got annoyed the one time I snogged a boy who was sort of attractive: 'But why would he kiss you?'

We were best friends because that was what had been decided when we were 13. I thought that made it law. I thought that made it forever. When we were 21 we moved into a flat together. If my friend saw mess anywhere, an old envelope or sandwich packet, she would not throw it into the bin but into my cupboard-sized room. Guess how that made me feel.

When I left that flat, started a new job, made new friends, I felt like I was breathing fresh, clear air for the first time in years. So I tried to pull away, but it was not easy. 'You are my best friend, why are you doing this to me?' she would say. Eventually it dawned on me that I had a choice. I wrote to her and told her that she wasn't my best friend, that she wasn't even my friend, that I didn't like her because she was selfish and cruel. She did not reply. Ever.

She was just one sort of terrorist friend, the sort that wants all of you, to have you as a sidekick, always available to kick. There are other sorts, the ones that suck the life out of you with their demands and expectations, the ones that insist you feel as sad as they do, the ones who constantly criticise, the ones who are artists with guilt. Different shades of the same creature.

We make mistakes when we are young (and when we are old) about who is right for us. They are so shiny, these new people. So we let them into our lives and we start forging connections, and then, because we so quickly become nostalgic, we find it hard to let go. And it feels nice, doesn't it, when someone depends on you, even if they are depending on you so hard that they are crushing you.

Friendship is meant to make you feel better. If it doesn't, then it might be time to let go. Hopefully, starving the friendship of oxygen will help it gently drop away. Be polite, while not offering anything of yourself. But be prepared for it to get a bit fighty. If it does, go in with your fists raised. They will be so astounded to see this rare moment of ruthlessness that they will almost certainly retreat. And then, it's over. What a relief.

# Don't Be An Askhole

We all know an askhole or two who, with their askholic tendencies, manage somehow to dissolve our concern; to blow a hole through our emotional investment. They are our friends, these askholes, we care. Or, at least, we care until we are too exhausted, too well used to care anymore. 'Let me know how I can help' evolves towards 'Ask someone who gives a shit'.

Askholes are advice seekers. Fair enough. Except they tend to operate in various utterly infuriating ways. The first involves asking for counsel regarding some kind of crisis and then listening – apparently attentively – to the advice (informed by hard-won wisdom) that is delivered. Advice that is designed to be properly constructive. Advice that is doled out when we could be sleeping or internet shopping or exercising or finding solutions to our own problems. The askhole will then either ignore the advice or spend a further wasted window of time pointing out why we are wrong; why the advice is faulty, what we have misunderstood about the situation. So thanks for that. No good deed...

Askholes also have a tendency to ask for advice on top secret, highly classified, potentially explosive, incredibly confidential matters. And so we give it our best shot and then vow to take the problem to the grave. We may lie there late at night worrying about the askhole and their hush-hush predicament. But soon, somehow, we will discover that the askhole has asked EVERYONE THEY HAVE EVER MET. So don't be an askhole. Because, by the time you are genuinely in trouble and you sincerely need guidance, you'll be talking to the hand.

# 10 Backhanded Compliments

You know the kind. Where someone says something that sounds nice. Until you think about it and realise you have just been gently insulted.

### 1. 'It's Very You'
No one but you would be stupid enough to wear that. No one but you thinks that bag isn't hideous.

### 2. 'Interesting...'
It's not interesting. It's just ugly.

### 3. 'They're So Cheerful'
Look at the bright colours on your terrible trousers. You look like you should be presenting children's television.

**4. 'I Couldn't Get Away With It, But That Haircut Really Suits You'**
You look terrible. And your head looks massive.

**5. 'I Love How Discerning You Are'**
No one wants to go out with you because you're horrible and for God's sake just order from the menu like a normal person.

**6. 'You Prefer To Look Natural, Don't You?'**
Put some mascara on. And get a wax before we all suffocate in the forest of your body hair.

**7. 'You Look Summery'**
You're dressed like a slag. I can see your nipples through that top.

**8. 'It's Such A Relief To Be On A Date With Someone Who Isn't Vain'**
We will not be going home together tonight because I do not fancy you.

**9. 'What I Like About You Is That You Always Have An Opinion'**
You opinionated royal pain in the arse.

**10. 'You Look So Healthy'**
Fatty.

## Are You Penis Pals?

As the saying goes: you can choose your friends, but you can't choose your…penis pals. Ah, you might wonder, what is a penis pal? Well, I'm glad you asked. A penis pal is a woman (or man) who has had sex with the same man you have had sex with. In other words, you have met the same penis. Ergo, penis pals.

This is rarely an edifying conceit. If it's your best friend then it's all a bit much. Bonding but, simultaneously, distancing. Particularly if it was a great love for one or the other of you. It never quite feels like 'family' but, rather, 'incest'. Of a kind. But we wear this slight shudder lightly because we've all been around the block a bit by this point so…it happens.

The troubling bit happens when you realise that you are penis pals with someone you either loathe or find incredibly mad or just disconcerting. Or when it's a woman who you know represents your direct competition in the singles market (sheesh) and who won't just…go away. Disappear. Get married or move abroad or something similarly helpful. How does one view it when a man who wants to fuck you has also wanted to fuck someone who – to your mind – no one should want to fuck.

We are not saying this is kind or reasonable or sane. But there are things about sex and sexual politics that are not kind or reasonable or sane. Things that press buttons. Things that niggle. Even though, let's be honest, there can be some nutrition in bonding over a total tool who's been mean to both of you. Who was 'hung like a shrimp and bad in bed'. Not that we would ever say that. Because it is not kind or reasonable or sane.

The best and darkest kind of penis pal is where you know that the two of you are pals but she doesn't. Evil. But true.

**Chapter 12**

# CLIMB EVERY MOUNTAIN

## (but my knee...)

IN THE OLDEN, GOLDEN DAYS, when our livers were plump and pink and we had a full deck of brain cells, when we were still in sleep surfeit because of amassed lie-ins, Going Out felt different. We didn't think about tomorrow, we only thought about tonight. And the best bit was the anticipation, the not-knowing, a feeling that buzzed in our chests as we applied thick, black liquid eyeliner, drinking home-made cosmopolitans, Kiss FM turned up loud. How would it all turn out? Where and who might we be at 3am? What adventures would be had? Who would we kiss? Who would we infuriate? Who would we meet on the night bus? Who knew? Brilliant.

But the universe expands, the world revolves, and although we humans gain much in emotional experience as we expand and revolve, we lose just as much in party stamina. Something shifts, imperceptibly at first, slowly and then all of a sudden. We start thinking about tomorrow.

It might have something to do with the realisation that there are no longer an infinite number of days available, and so to spend a whole one vomiting/napping/eating all the dim sum is perhaps a bit of a shame. But the basic problem is that after a certain amount of use a liver just can't hack it anymore, so that even two and a half glasses of wine with dinner has consequences. And two bottles of red wine with nothing but a few peanuts results in a total body and mind Armageddon, the shockwaves of which can still be felt three days later.

There are, of course, a few party beasts who do not seem to experience this shift, who remain as committed at 49 as they were at 22; but while they were once the life-and-soul of all our house parties, air-guitaring in their high heels on the sofa and drinking warm prosecco from the bottle, they are now a little terrifying, especially when it is 3am and they are still in your house, spraying cocaine around your bathroom even though everyone else has gone home and it was only a gentle weekday dinner in the first place.

But these are rare animals. Most of us are the opposite of the party beast, and that has its own dangers, because we become obsessed with tomorrow before tonight has even begun. As we stand in front of the mirror, applying concealer, drinking a vodka and tonic, listening to Prince, our chests no longer buzz with anticipation, they thrum with fear. How long will I have to stay? Who will be there? Will I have to talk to that boring woman I always feel the need to impress? Will I catch someone's cold?

Will I fall over in these stupid shoes? Will I burn the roof of my mouth with a honey-glazed chipolata? Will I have to dance? Will I be able to get home? Will I be in bed by midnight? Will I cope tomorrow?

Really, the question is merely mathematical: how much fun can I have without feeling unacceptably appalling tomorrow? The fun/dysfunction ratio is an equation that each person must work out for themselves; it takes practice and refinement and is subject to change. The dial moves along (sadly).

But there are unexpected miracles, like the Thursday night when you think fuck it and accept the last-minute invitation to the random thing and have four glasses of cold champagne and a perfect martini, a couple of sneaky fags, maybe even a micro-flirt and then next day you wake up and…Nothing! Fresh as a fucking daisy. You even look good, sort of happy and glowy. How did that happen? No one knows. It is one of the mysteries of the Midult universe, but one only experienced by those who, now and again, let themselves forget about tomorrow.

## The Moment We Leave The House

1. Is the steamer off? Even though I know I haven't used the steamer for about two years. But is it off?
2. Have I got my phone? *starts rattling bag, patting clothes, swearing, physically shaking*
3. I loathe what I am wearing. Is it too late to go and change? [It is.] What was I thinking attempting this boho executive thing? Execu-ho. I look ridiculous.
4. I need the loo. What's *wrong* with me?
5. I am not going to eat bread all day. No need to eat bread. I do not even want bread. Bread is not so special. I am hungry.
6. Startlingly unexpected sex thought about neighbour/postman/John Humphrys. *Cheers up*.
7. Is it going to be OK? Am I going to be OK? Can I do this? Is it possible? Does anyone know if it's possible? Does Brian Cox know? Does Susanna Reid know?
8. Is today the day I'll be burgled?
9. My bra hurts.
10. What am I going to have for dinner?

## How To Get Out Of Almost Anything

### Claustrophobia

Is there anything more useful? This will get you out of camping, caravanning, the

Underground, sharing a bed, sitting in the middle of a banquette, changing rooms, leggings, big queues, complicated underwear. 'I'm claustrophobic.' That's all.

## The Dog
I can't leave the dog/bring the dog/sorry, the dog. The dog, the dog. And if I do come, all I will talk about is the dog. The dog, the dog. So sorry. The dog. (You will become so boring about the dog no one will want to hang out with you but that's OK because then it can be just you and the dog.)

## Allergies
Gosh, you look a little stressed/teary/mental asks a concerned someone. 'It's just my allergies.' Not 'I am having a mini breakdown, can't sleep, hate all my clothes, mislaid my phone for at least a second and have been crying on and off for weeks.' See? 'Allergies' is better.

## IBS
Sorry I can't eat your complicated dinner/all those carbs/go to that restaurant/eat out/ go out/see anyone ever again. It's my IBS.

## Novel
I have to work on my novel. I've done 35,000 words/almost finished the third draft/am deep, deep into the story arc/feel I need to sit and really inhabit the characters. Frankly, after this, no one will want to see you anyway.

## Mercury Is In Retrograde
So I can't make any big decisions, otherwise the universe will slam me down. Whether or not you believe in horoscopes, Mercury is a bastard.

## Hormones
Pre-hormonal, during-hormonal, post-hormonal, perimenopausal, actually menopausal, full moon hormonal, totally out of your sodding mind hormonal. Flash your period tracker app or send a screen grab at someone saying, 'See, see, see.' No one 'really' understands what they are looking at, so watch as your evening/lunch/ workout vanishes into blissfully thin air. Your time is now your own. Enjoy the sofa. You are welcome.

# Conversations You Have With Yourself In The Car

Me:        This traffic though.

Also me:  BEEP THE HORN SPEED THESE BASTARDS UP.

Me:        At least I can listen to *Woman's Hour* while I'm stuck here.

Also me:  WHY IS THE PERSON IN FRONT LEAVING THAT BIG GAP IN FRONT OF THEM FOR NO REASON HURRY THE FUCK UP MOTHERFUCKER.

Me:        This play about sexual harassment that Jenni Murray is talking about sounds harrowing but important.

Also me:  THIS STUPID TWAT IN FRONT OF ME DOES NOT KNOW WHERE HE IS GOING GET THE FUCK OUT OF MY WAY YOU FUCKING FUCK.

Me:        I must remember to talk to my mother about how she gets her orchid to keep reflowering.

Also me:  HE'S LOOKING AT A FUCKING SAT NAV I MIGHT HAVE KNOWN MY RAGE JUST WENT UP TO 20 OUT OF 10 PULL OVER IF YOU DON'T KNOW WHERE YOU'RE GOING DON'T CRAWL AT 12 MILES AN HOUR.

Me:        Rats, I forgot to take my washing out of the machine before I left. Oh well.

Also me:  SERIOUSLY HOW DID THIS PERSON GET A LICENCE? A MONKEY COULD DRIVE BETTER THAN THIS. WHY DO PEOPLE NOT OBSERVE THE SPEED LIMIT? ARE YOU ILL?

Me:        Might knock off early today. Bit tired.

Also me:  STOP TRYING TO HAVE A CONVERSATION WITH THE PERSON IN THE PASSENGER SEAT AND FOCUS ON THE ROAD OR I WILL CUT YOU.

Me:        I could catch up with *The Apprentice* and then go to bed early.

Also me:  WHO IS THIS DICKHEAD DRIVING RIGHT UP MY ARSE? RIGHT I WILL SLOW DOWN DELIBERATELY TO TEACH YOU A LESSON YOU STUPID FUCK.

Me:        Might just get a takeaway too.

Also me:  WHO IS THIS FUCKING MORON IN FRONT WHO IS COMING TO A GRINDING HALT JUST BECAUSE THERE ARE SPEEDBUMPS? ARE YOU MADE OF FUCKING GLASS OR SOMETHING? GROW UP YOU BIG FUCKING BABY.

Me:        Mustn't forget to do my peace and gratitude affirmations when I get home.

Also me:  Literally never been happier.

# Am I An Alcoholic?

Oh, probably. If you're reading this then there's clearly an echo of...something suspicious. Let me ask you some questions: do you ever lie to your friends about how much you had to drink or how often you drink? I do. Fairly normal, no? Do you ever lie to your shrink about it? Problematic.

The trouble is, how to establish the rules when the government directives are so municipal and so unrelated to real life and galvanise the inner rebel in even the most bovine of us? Units. Who counts units?

Let's try to have a look at this: more than two drinks when on your own is a bit of a flare in the night sky, especially if it happens more than once in a blood blue super moon. And memory loss, I'm afraid, means it's time to calm the fuck down because it's a sign of the brain doing something sinister. Can't remember what. Know it's not good.

Having sex with people without meaning to is bad enough as a teenager and worse as, say, a single Midult mother. Or a married Midult mother. Or a single Midult looking for someone. Or a single Midult not even that bothered about finding someone. Unintentional sex that you can't remember is depressing.

The scariest ones are the machines who don't get hangovers. They can hurtle towards 50, lunchtime drinking and Thursday–Sunday snorting, all the while holding down big jobs and marriages. They are rare and die young.

As a borderline alcoholic I do deals with myself. I plan big nights so that they in no way affect my day-to-day life. Friday night only. With trusted friends. Fully functional stuff. Just don't tell my shrink. She'll say something annoying like, 'Why do you feel the need to not be present?' Frankly it's none of her business.

# Alcohol Vs. Coffee

Alcohol:  I don't want to sound cocky – but it's me.
Coffee:   Wrong.
Alcohol:  I'm the thing she wants at the end of the day.
Coffee:   And I'm the thing she NEEDS first thing in the morning.
Alcohol:  That's dependency, not love.
Coffee:   You're allowed to need someone, you know.
Alcohol:  So unsexy.
Coffee:   It's called being in an adult relationship, actually.
Alcohol:  I make her feel sexy.
Coffee:   I make her feel awake. You can't feel sexy if you're not conscious.
Alcohol:  I make her feel relaxed.

| | |
|---|---|
| Coffee: | I make her feel competent. |
| Alcohol: | She lets go because of me. |
| Coffee: | (in a tiny voice) And acts like a dick. |
| Alcohol: | What was that? |
| Coffee: | You heard. |
| Alcohol: | OK, so she acts like a dick – it's funny though. |
| Coffee: | That's debatable. |
| Alcohol: | She enjoys me. |
| Coffee: | She enjoys me. And I don't make her feel like shit afterwards. |
| Alcohol: | You make her grumpy and give her headaches. |
| Coffee: | So do you. |
| Alcohol: | That's true, actually… |
| Coffee: | Maybe we're both a bit… |
| Alcohol: | Yeah… |
| Coffee: | I liked it that time you made her do the splits in the middle of her parents' ruby wedding anniversary. |
| Alcohol: | That was funny. And she really needed you the next day. |
| Coffee: | Exactly! |
| Alcohol: | We make a good team. |
| Coffee: | Good point well made. |
| Alcohol: | You do make her teeth a weird colour though. |
| Coffee: | And you make her dance badly. |
| Alcohol: | At least she wants to dance with me. |
| Coffee: | The flailing arms, the swinging head, that baffling knee-jerking movement. It's embarrassing. |
| Alcohol: | It's called 'having a good time' you moron. |
| Coffee: | You always leave me to pick up the pieces. |
| Alcohol: | Oh, excuse me, your royal burning martyrness. |
| Coffee: | She can't operate heavy machinery after you! |
| Alcohol: | I can live with that. |

## The Psychology Of Ordering

Welcome to the psychology of ordering. Because there is one. And it kicks in most acutely the moment we go out to lunch or dinner with other women. Does the following sound familiar?

'What do you feel like?' *looks shiftily from menu to friend and back again*

'Hmmm…I haven't even looked, actually [Narrator: she had totally already looked]...What are you having?' *looks nervously from friend to menu and back again*

There is so much at play here; so much revolving around our relationship with food and competition and perception. It all begins with bread. Will you? Should I? Can I? Will I ever forgive myself? Is this a blowout? If I have bread do I need to have salad afterwards or is bread the key to the floodgates? Does bread clear the path for chips and pudding? I can't be the first to have bread. Or, if I am the first, will the others just stare at me or will they all dive into the lovely bread sea?

And, moving on, imagine the horror of ordering a starter when no one else does. And, conversely, imagine the horror of not ordering a starter when everyone else does and then feeling ravenous and jealous. And resentful. And ravenous.

And if I order the sashimi and you order the noodles then will I feel virtuous and thin or hungry and cross because, what I really want, is the sashimi *and* the noodles. Also my wine is almost finished and everyone else has had one sip.

None of this is about judging others on what they eat. We are too grown-up for that. It is all about having our needs met while trying to establish the food mood of the crowd. Generally we say, fuck it. But if we've – slightly unintentionally – ended up with broth while everyone else has had pizza then we might not feel so thrilled. But perhaps vice versa is worse. Which is why, you will notice, that women in groups will tend to order with the same vibe. For balance. To fit in. To form a funny food team. To not feel gluttonous or deprived.

## All The Dinner Parties We've Been To

### The One At University
On the menu: pasta with pesto from a jar and a bag of salad. Motivation: aren't we sophisticated having a dinner party with £3 bottles of wine? Then off to the pub for snakebite and black. Then back to the filthy flat for terrible sex on the kitchen table, because you'd read somewhere that this is what you should do if you are 'wild', and one of your flatmates walks in, which kind of killed the whole 'kitchen supper' thing before it had even started.

### The One Where You Threw Up In The Loo
You are invited to a dinner party by a slightly older friend, in somewhere a bit smarter than where you live. They are all composers and artists and overwhelm you – well that's your excuse anyway. You drink so much red wine that you throw up all ALL over the bathroom in a scene from *The Exorcist*. They call you a cab. MORTIFICATION. And now you live quite near and cannot go past the house without a wave of nausea/shame hitting you 20 years on.

### The One That Turned Into A Kitchen Rave

A smart little dinner with just a few brilliant people, two of whom you have never met before but immediately adore. The host does their 'signature' chicken/mozzarella/Parma ham thing. With mashed potato and this new phenomenon called Tenderstem broccoli. Two days later you are still up and buying magic mushrooms from Portobello Market.

### The One With A New Boyfriend

Oh come and look at my new boyfriend/new sofa. Isn't he/it lovely? Look at those legs, the frame, so hard. He/It's probably/definitely the one. (He wasn't. Neither was the sofa. Bastards.)

### The One Where There Was No Food

Come they said. 8pm. Bring a bottle. And there are some crisps. But by 9pm you have noticed two things. No one is cooking. You are starving. No one looks bothered. They are too busy talking. Wow, they can talk. Did you miss something? Was this not a dinner party?

### The One Where You Kissed A Boy You Really Didn't Mean To Kiss

A grown-up girl has invited you to a grown-up dinner, with posh cutlery and napkins and three courses. Please behave, please behave. Instead you kiss a guy you really didn't fancy in the room where all the coats are. Years later you bump into this guy and he says, 'Hey I remember you, you were at that dinner party where I kissed the really drunk girl in the room with all the coats.' You say NOTHING.

### The One With Work Friends

You are so thrilled, so in love, so excited with your work friends, they are so clever and brilliant and you know you are going spend the rest of your life with them. As a result you get totally overexcited and end up flashing your newly Brazilianed bits. They say your pubes look like Hitler's moustache. Fifteen years later you set up a business together.

### The One With Foodies

'We're foodies,' they say fake apologetically as they offer you some kind of cod's roe monstrosity. 'We're just hopeless foodies,' they hoot as they spoon out some fermented soy bean thing on top of blue beef and terrifying-looking mushrooms covered in foam. There are many, many different wines. You are so confused. 'Terrible foodies,' they squawk over homemade baklava that somehow tastes of soap. You get home and comfort eat Crunchy Nut.

### The One Where You Have An Unexpectedly Nice Moment
You are so nervous going to this strange person who has invited you to dinner's house. You take a minicab and you are wearing a new dress that no one has seen, not even your mother, and for some reason that makes you feel crushingly lonely. But you are going to this dinner party because how else will you meet The One? The One isn't there, but there's a lovely girl so you huddle in the corner all night laughing like drains and you think maybe you've made a friend for life. You never see her again.

### The One Where You Cooked Something Delicious…
…and then someone brought a pudding and that is all anyone talked about and you are still not over it. So what if he's a chef? You will never forgive him. Or anyone who was there. Fuck the lot of them.

### The One With The Power Players
The hostess sends you a text on the morning of the dinner telling you who everyone is and what they do for a living/what books they have published. Before the food is served they insist on going round the table to ask everyone to state their topline agenda for sustainable business and before pudding they go around again asking everyone what they are grateful for. You find another human being, smoke a joint out of the loo window and then experience an appalling paranoid episode.

### The One Where You Were In Love At The Beginning And Then Weren't
It's all going swimmingly, isn't it? You are sitting opposite your boyfriend, and he has just asked for the pepper. You feel that repulsed heat travelling over your body and your stomach feels like it is falling out and you go into the bathroom and you look in the mirror and you know: it's not going to work out. Obviously you don't tell him for another three years.

### The One With The Set-Up
Everyone knows. And the moment you walk into the room you know that this has been badly misjudged. He is wearing a fleece. It is a very trying evening…for both of you. You bump into each other at a thing a few weeks later and cannot bear to say hello.

### The One With New Couple Friends Who Turn Out To Be Alcoholics
It's a Tuesday. You are hoping they will turn up at 7.30. They weave in at 8.55 because they 'popped into the pub for a quickie'. They bring four bottles with them which is… generous? You call them a cab at 1.05am because their lips have turned blue and they are rootling through cupboards looking for…what? Lighter fluid?

# The Seven-Minute Party Plan

Parties!!! Woohoo!!! Or perhaps: Parties!!! Boohoo!!! Depends on the mood, depends on the party. Drinks parties in particular are disheartening. Why do people have them? What can a drinks party possibly add to the fun index of life? What is fun about standing around with no beginning or end to shape the proceedings, looking over people's shoulders? No one yet has been able to explain the point.

But when duty calls, while spirits are sagging, there is a way to swerve the full-blown horror of the standing about trying to avoid repeated cases of 'The Awkwards'. Welcome to the Seven-Minute Party Plan. Here is the essence of it: keep moving at all times. Never stand still.

- Arrive exactly one hour after the invitation says the party begins. It will be at its fullest and most chaotic, which – for your evil purposes – is good news.
- Each conversation has a beginning, middle and an end.
- Beginning: 'It's SO nice to see you...I was just thinking about the time that...'
- Middle: Incredibly brief observation about anything at all. Could be a compliment or a joke or something political or something scandalous.
- End: 'Back in a sec. I must just go to the loo/get a drink/say hello to/make a call.'
- You do one round of the room in this way and you are almost oppressively cheerful but constantly in motion while talking.
- Leave. No goodbyes (particularly not to the host). Just dissolve into the night. Your presence will have been noted, your exit will not register.

Do not forget: movement, smiling, circle the room, invisible evaporation. And a follow-up text saying how nice it was to see everyone. You will be in and out in no less than seven, no more than nine minutes. This way it hardly hurts at all.

# Girl Manterrupted

Sometimes it's as though you're not there. You have a voice only dogs can hear, perhaps. Or, maybe, when your lovely lady-voice starts tinkling, they hear a monkey clapping in their heads. Manterrupters happen. Here are some things to say that might confuse them a little. Poor them. Ish.

1. You know it's true love when the other person finishes your sentences for you.
2. Can you say that again, but slower – maybe at the speed a unicorn would trot at. Do you love unicorns too?
3. How many times did you think about sex while you were saying that?

4.  That's great – if you could now rescue me from my tower and validate my existence by asking me to marry you, I'd be grateful.
5.  I don't understand what you're saying. That's because it's not pink.
6.  Did you hear that noise? It's the sound of my soul screaming.
7.  You're adorable, do you know that?
8.  We can't go any further in this conversation until you can tell me the name of Bette Midler's character in *Beaches*. Only then will I know I can trust you.
9.  Shall we do a selfie?
10. It's OK, I know I'm good at driving because after I gave my driving instructor a blow job, he said I was the best pupil he'd ever had. Thanks for the helpful parking tips though.
11. I'd like to settle this with a game of French skipping.
12. That was so impressive. Again! Again!
13. I might go and have a little lie down while you finish my thought process.

## The Horror Of Bumping Into Someone You Shagged

So you go to a wedding, and you bump into a boy/man you went to university with. And all the time you are saying in front of partners/parents/priests, etc. 'Remember that professor who had a thing about split infinitives?' you are also thinking about the fact you had sex with this man/boy. A lot of sex. In fact, you banged him in the halls of residence communal laundry room, in the student union loo, over the wall at the bottom of the sports fields, behind the tent at the summer ball. Who was that girl? And why are you now having to deal with her banging?

Or maybe you are at a book launch and the first person you see is someone you had a one-night stand with (you may have shagged him a second time, who knows? You were drunk) and ended up in a Hilton hotel and had to go to work dressed in the same clothes and everyone knew and you didn't care because you were only 25 and you felt like a bad-ass. And there's that time at a 40th where you walk in only to find that you've had sex with three of the people round the (very large) table.

My sexual past keeps popping up and it's beginning to feel harder and harder to deal with. Because someone else slept with those people, an entirely different human with different skin and body and hair. It was 20 years ago. And so why am *I* having to pick up the pieces via these incredibly awkward conversations?

Back at the book launch, the boy/man's wife is there and we end up looking at pictures of his children (my fault for asking), which is oddly weird because I am having a 20-year sex flashback at the time. What is a 20-year-old flashback like? Hazy, naked. AARGH did we have to be naked? He ran me a bath. Oof.

And now I am never going to leave the house again because out in the world there are thousands of people (not *thousands* Mum, obviously) who have seen a 20-something girl without her clothes on and this 40-something woman is NOT HAPPY ABOUT IT.

## What's Your Drunk Personality?

Same woman. Same booze. Different effects. Welcome to the lottery of drunkenness, the chocolate box of drunkenness, the Russian roulette of drunkenness. Who knows what tonight will bring...

### Drunk And On Electrifying Form

The unicorn of drunkenness – where you actually turn into a Netflix comedy hit version of yourself, regaling the room with sensational stories, fuelled by your alcohol-charged confidence. You're the person who suggests the hilarious games, who starts the dancing, who will make a tit of themselves in a way that is nothing but charming and self-deprecating. You are the delightful drunk, impressing everyone with your well-timed jokes and winning outrageousness.

### Drunk And Crying

The crying will inevitably start with a self-indulgent statement that no one can answer without making the tears worse: 'You all think I'm a twat.'/'You're all so much more successful than me.'/'I never had piano lessons when I was little, like my sister did, and now she's married and I'm not.' It's like you've let all your demons out of the cave at once and have offered yourself up to the room for a therapy session they want no part in. Someone should take you home.

### Drunk And Touchy

Sometimes you get drunk and just want to pick a fight. Everything sounds inflammatory to you, which makes you deliberately provocative and immediately argumentative. You are suddenly the one who wants to unpick every sentence: 'Wait, what do you MEAN by that?' and will find offence in something as innocuous as being told you look good tonight: 'Oh, I look good "tonight", do I? Because, what? I usually look like shit?' Harder to navigate than a field full of mines.

**Drunk And Accidentally At A Cultural Event**
Suddenly the naked willies in the art are the funniest thing you've ever seen IN. YOUR. LIFE.

**Drunk And Tired**
When Cinderella syndrome strikes you feel you must vacate the premises immediately. You might be in the middle of a conversation where you just get up and leave with your interlocutor trailing off in mid-sentence. You might manage to fumble out 'I can't be here', at best, but it's the kind of moment where manners abandon you and home magically calls like Mr Rochester to Jane Eyre across the moors. You must obey before you go to sleep standing up, like a horse.

**So Drunk You're Imperceptibly Drunk**
The strange, almost celestial stillness that accompanies the truly drunk. It's like your brain has been bundled off to a locked room while your body goes into code-red crisis talks about what to do with you. While all this goes on, you take on the appearance of someone strangely normal and calm. Sweet and inoffensive, patient and easy-going – as if life just became incredibly simple.

# How To Own The Photo Booth

A party's not a party without a photo booth. You can't move for photo booths. But they are excellent things. Firstly, they are never not fun. Secondly, they calm people down in terms of documenting the arse out of the evening. So phones stay in bags a bit more, which has to be a good thing.

Photo booths are bond-y, flirty, cosy and – crucially – flattering. Really, really flattering. I guess they use a ring flash or Vaseline or some such. The ones with the wind machine are like having your own personal director of photography. It's actually quite hard to get a bad picture. Which means you take armfuls of them home and display them 'casually'. Who actually prints iPhone pictures? Or any pictures? Photo booths might be the only way...

Here are some tips from a Midult booth bitch:

1. Damn well concentrate. Everyone else is drunk. You can be drunk but with one brain cell focused on when the thing is actually going to flash.
2. Slip your shoulders behind your booth partner so you look less broad. Similarly, sit at the back of the group so you don't get a looming moon face in the print. Reverse if very narrow and pin-headed.

3. A kiss pose is fab for the jawline. If this is a cheek-kiss, be the kisser rather than the kissee who usually looks a bit gormless.
4. Booth bomb: wait until the final moment, burst through the curtain and interrupt another booth session. Slightly daring and faintly witty. Every little helps.
5. Be quick off the mark to snaffle the print – that way you are IN CONTROL. You can tear it up if it's rubbish, blow it up if it's gorgeous. Phew.

# Home And Drunk

We used to worry about the snogging and the smoking, but these days? Well, have you ever stopped to think about the odd and pointless things you do when you get home drunk?

### Drunk Trying-On
Now, you think, is the most absolutely perfect time to be trying on those party dresses you haven't worn in ten years. Ooopsy! Fell over trying to do the zip. Whoops – bit stuck in this one. The next morning you wake up half-in, half-out of a really bad bridesmaid's dress. When you stand up you realise you took some shears to it at two in the morning to turn it from maxi to midi. Amazing you didn't lose a finger, really. But does it miraculously work now? It does not.

### Drunk Bath Running
'Baths are the best!' is the last thing you think before you pass out. You wake up and realise that you ran it but you didn't get in it. You used all your nice eye-wateringly expensive bath oil. And now there's just a grey ring around the tub full of cold, grey water. A metaphor for your hangover. But thank God you turned it off.

### Drunk Pedicure
Your toes were like little cherries and they looked lovely, but now the pedicure is old and your feet look like you've stubbed your toes many, many times (maybe you have). So you get home and you just know that this is the perfect time to take it off. You can't find any cotton pads so grab the loo roll. In the morning the bathroom looks like you've murdered someone in it. (Have you?)

### Drunk Instagramming
You are on a spree, wheeeee, look at your thumb whirring away, liking everything from the accounts of celebrities (Kate Beckinsale, Reese Witherspoon, Millie Bobby Brown, like like like), to all your friends and then all your 'friends' and then random people

you don't know in the 'you might like this section'. And you comment, why not? 'Love this', 'Great', 'Fabulous', while simultaneously sharing all the memes with your work wife. 'Us', 'Me', 'You', '#same'. You wake up to 55 very nervous-making notifications.

### Drunk Tinder Cruising
You are single but you shouldn't be because you are so totally gorgeous. And for once, drunk, you believe it. So off you go, swiping right, starting conversations, sending emojis, putting yourself out there. It's good, right? It's positive, yes?

### Drunk And Pointless Reading
As you get into bed you wriggle down and grab your improving book – so good, so clever – and wake up with it mashed under your head, dribbled over and who knows if you've read anything. In fact, you've never seen this book in your life. Who bought the book? And why?

### Drunk List-Making
It is all perfectly clear. Everything makes sense. You have found the key to your universe, the opening lines of your novel, the beginning of the screenplay you've been dreaming of writing, the mantra to live by. In the morning the notes read 'rtirgjsfbnsgerjogjslca;;cmjsjvrlgjisoplvn.x'.

### Drunk Eating The Fridge
You were hungry.

## All The Hangovers We've Had

### The Cold Sweats Hangover
When you wake up shivering like you were a baby that has been left exposed on a mountainside and then realise you have lost your body heat through unstoppable sweating that has now saturated your sheets and has turned cold, making you damp and freezing. The last thing you can remember from last night is getting into a cupboard with someone and starting to swap clothes. Presumably that's why you're wearing a man-sized hoodie and some boxer shorts...

### The Paranoid Hangover
Holy Christ. What did you say last night? Did you tell anyone about your best friend's husband coming on to you that time? Did you tell them about what a bitch you think your sister-in-law is? Did you tell that story about shagging two different men in a

24-hour period? Or when you did coke with that guy from *Hollyoaks* who you then snogged because you thought he was actually someone else? Was everyone laughing at you? NEVER, EVER GO OUT AND MIX WITH OTHER HUMANS AGAIN.

### The Exhausted But Can't Sleep Hangover
You've gone to bed pissed but are now only sleeping in 20-minute bursts, effectively staying awake to witness your drunkenness turning into a hangover.

### The Unquenchable Hangover
Got a mouth like a hay bale. Must flush out the poison with water. Why is none of it being absorbed? Can feel organs turning to crisp packets. Brain is literally shrinking from lack of moisture. More water. Aargh, now need to pee for the 20th time. Why didn't you get more coconut water?? Does Lucozade actually work? Is now the time to start drinking Coke again?

### The Waking Up Giggling Hangover
You mistakenly ate a kipper, slapped your best friend, got thrown out of a nightclub for trying to climb over the bar to show the barman how to make a proper martini, spent the whole of the night bus journey home singing Barbra Streisand songs and everyone on the top deck had joined in. You call your friend the moment you wake up and she picks up; neither of you speak, you both just laugh until someone says 'Kipper!'

### The I Am Actually Still Drunk Hangover
The last thing you remember was when someone wrestled you to the ground and poured expensive vodka into your eyeballs because she had read somewhere that this is the most effective way to absorb alcohol. And now it is 9.30am and you are sitting in a heads of department meeting. You have chosen a seat close to the door in case you need to make a run for it, your hair still smells of vodka, and when the CEO says, 'So, there have been some successful movements this year,' you write the word 'bowel' on your notepad and push it across to Jean from marketing.

### The Two-Day Hangover
You anticipated Sunday. Let's not even talk about Sunday. But now it is 3pm on Monday and your brain feels shrivelled, your hands shake, you self-medicated with lasagne and chips for lunch and you are still doing tequila burps. You worry that you have done something irrevocable to your body and you will feel like this FOR THE REST OF YOUR LIFE.

# Cation-Ary Tales

### Exfoli-Cation
Fly somewhere like Turkey to be totally cleansed inside and out. Stripped of all the bad juju, exfoliated to hell and back, starved and pummelled and lectured. Wall-to-wall enemas. Back-to-back hikes. So slim and serene. Have some Pringles and one glass of wine on the easyJet flight back home and try to start a fight.

### No-Cation
If you can see a child or hear a child, let alone have to speak to a child, it's a no-cation.

### The Make-Or-Break-Cation
It's been so long since you've had sex that you can't remember your pet name for his penis. Perhaps that pet name is the problem. You wax, he trims. You floss, he shaves. This is all a bit embarrassing. Best get drunk.

### The Man-Cation
For men, with other men, doing a manly activity like golf or fishing or walking. What could be more manly than hanging out with other men? How heterosexual is that? Particularly if there is some naked lake swimming involved. And playfighting. And much meat.

### Yolo-Cation
See you at the Grand Canyon/Angkor Wat/the Inca Trail. Or maybe Burning Man. You are not a tourist. Oh no, you are a traveller. You might even be an explorer. You are broadening your horizons and flirting (very, very, very lightly) with death. You camp in rainforest villages/mountain villages/rural villages and eat strange local stews. You take coloured pencils for the children. You are a citizen of the world. You spend the last three nights in the best hotel you can afford, wondering if you've got that tick that swims up your pee-stream into your bits.

### Solo-Cation
Who are you? Who knows? Maybe a weekend alone up a mountain will help. No one can hear you scream.

### The School-Cation
You go to Paris for a history of art tour, but the whole thing descends into a St Trinian's-esque storm, nearly giving your already-on-edge teacher a heart attack. Every night

you all get wildly drunk, everyone chain-smokes, you try (and largely fail) to pick up local boys and you get locked out of the hotel at 1am. Your teacher wakes up for weeks after the trip, shouting, 'WHERE ARE THEY? WHERE ARE THEY?' and has to be physically restrained by his wife.

### Sleep-Cation

Extraordinarily tired? How about putting yourself in a controlled coma for the weekend. Dignitas-lite.

### The Sex-Cation

The first holiday with a new boyfriend. Sex, sex, more sex, then more sex. Not leaving the hotel until you'd had sex about four times before lunch. Not really seeing or doing anything as a result. Both feeling sick because you'd had too much sex. Unable to stop having sex though. Is he a bit annoying? Better have more sex to find out.

### Cry-Cation

When you howl at the moon, throw yourself against the wall, rend your garments and then propose to yourself on the beach. It happens.

### Edu-Cation

Involving guidebooks, comfortable shoes and even a journal. Possibly a backpack. You'll be lighting a lot of candles and praying to the mummified holy foreskin of St Moritz in Prague.

### The Girl-Cation

You all pile into someone's mother's house somewhere in Italy and it's going to be so amazing and 'I'm packing really light, are you?' No one can lift their case. Two of you fancy the same boy next door so you keep pretending to go to bed early and then bump into each other – fully made up – peering over the fence in some kind of horrific baby doll nightie. One girl catches everyone bitching about her and cries boringly for two whole days – but the biggest tragedy is when it's cloudy for half an hour during which time you all pluck all of your eyebrows off.

## What's In Your Running Away Bag?

The world has gone mad. You never know when you might need to cut loose and get off the bus. These are our Midult running away supplies. Frankly, this is what our holiday suitcase looks like too...

## 1. Your Phone Charger

If your phone dies, you die. Be practical. How else will you Instagram-story your tragic descent into madness?

## 2. Your Favourite Pillow

Laughable, given that you will not be sleeping ever again at this rate, but at least you can keep up the pretence of attempting to with something comfortable and comforting.

## 3. A Picture Of Justin Trudeau

Take the one of him balancing on the side of a table to demonstrate how strong his core is. Or the one of him stroking a baby's face – or at Canadian Pride – or boxing, so you can see his tattoos. It will really cheer you up.

## 4. Tweezers

For chin hairs. Can double as a weapon.

## 5. A Bag Of Xanax

There's no need to be mentally present for all of this, you know.

## 6. Bread

If not now, when???

## 7. A Hot Water Bottle

Who doesn't feel better with a nice, toasty hot water bottle gently generating heat up their jumper?

## 8. An Unreasonable Amount Of Clean Knickers

No matter how desperate life gets, there are some things that can't be compromised on.

## 9. Interdental Sticks

Especially if there's going to be foraging. All those nuts and berries and grubs. (Clearly we have some sort of Mowgli fantasy going on here.)

## 10. SPF

Can't deal with any more age spots.

## 24 Things You Only Know Once You've Moved To The Country

1. You think nothing of cooking supper with your knickers drying all over the Aga.
2. You don't know your neighbours because you can't find them.
3. A clutch is NOT a crucial accessory when you go out for the evening. Wellies and a head torch are.
4. Long-life milk still exists and it's in your food cupboard. Sorry. Larder.
5. Taxis are not a spontaneous event. The local cab must be booked at least two weeks in advance. *deletes Uber app...weeps*
6. The phone ringing no longer sparks dread. You long for the thing to ring. Even if it's PPI. It's still a voice.
7. Ambushing the postman is a daily sport. You can force at least five minutes' chat out of him before he makes a break for it.
8. You check coffee supplies more than you check Instagram (it's a 30-minute round trip to the nearest shop y'know).
9. You're an eco-fraud. Yes, you've spent years worrying about air and road miles. Now? Not so much. If Prime can deliver, you're good.
10. Talking to yourself is no longer acceptable. With all this silence in the countryside it feels too much like A SIGN.
11. People walk into your house unannounced. Before you hear them knock they're in your kitchen calling, 'Yoo-hoo!' Sometimes charming, sometimes alarming.
12. Homespun gifts are de rigueur. Eggs from the hens (SO prolific!), boxes of plums (we simply can't get through them all!), jam (from the last of the rasps). You MUST reciprocate. If desperate, steam labels off Bonne Maman and replace with wonkily written ones.
13. You spend more time than you'd like to admit thinking about post-and-rail fences and biomass boilers. WTF?
14. You will never have to parallel park again. *shudders with relief*
15. The DHD/Yodel man is monosyllabic because he hates you. He has just driven ten miles along single-track roads to deliver this small package that may or may not be a Pritt Stick.
16. The septic tank is an obsession. What if someone flushes the wrong thing? Should I laminate 'Polite Notice' signs? Do people on mains sewage even KNOW how lucky they are?
17. You only take your coat off when you go to bed.
18. People suggest a dog walk rather than coffee. When you say you don't have a dog they struggle to look you in the eye again.

19. You used to watch YouTube videos on plucking eyebrows. Now you watch ones on fucking (sorry – plucking) pheasants.
20. 75 per cent of your wardrobe is dead. Farewell slouchy jumpsuit. Swishy skirt. Anything in suede.
21. You must be handy at everything from tiling to tree planting. If you get-a-man-in, do so under cover of darkness and admit it to no one.
22. You judge all your townie friends on how helpful/charming/demanding they are as a house guest. And on the quality of goodies they bring.
23. The chap who delivers milk and eggs also stocks chocolate in his van. Who knew.
24. You can freeze pretty much anything. Nuts. Milk. Bananas. Egg. Oranges. Avocados. On this last point, you also need to make sure you get out more.

## Welcome to Midulthood

# ALTERNATIVE FACTS FOR MIDULTS

For when the truth is inconvenient...

1. He is, in fact, trapped under something heavy. That is why he hasn't called or texted. Trapped. Possibly underground.
2. Just as chewing gum gets your digestive juices flowing, thinking about exercise activates the muscles and ignites the metabolism.
3. Everything is secretly being printed in a smaller font to save money. You can see fine. Your eyesight is just as sharp as it always was.
4. Pizza is a salad.
5. Yoga leggings have a powerful subliminal effect on the male libido.
6. Extreme stress keeps you young. Remember what it was like being a teenager and you were 'like so totally stressed out about exams and boys and shit'? How young did you look then?
7. No one saw you parking. No one laughed.
8. Drinking this herbal tea not only will be a sensible substitute for caffeine, but it will also make you calmer and more able to deal with all the things that are coming your way, like not having filed your tax return yet. No need to panic or worry about anything: your tea has this.
9. You are not going grey. That's just a bit of blonde. You are a late-blooming blonde. This is a thing.

# Chapter 13

# PERFECTION? YOU CAN KEEP IT

I MET SOMEONE THE OTHER DAY who said that she was concerned with 'self-perfection'. She was incredibly preoccupied with doing everything right and being seen to do everything right. The right choices, the right name, the right time to get married, the right way to be as right and irreproachable as possible. The best way to be flawless. Correct. Admirable. And she wanted my advice, which in itself is funny because, however flattering the light, however aligned the planets and however rose-tinted the view, I am very, very not perfect.

I am also not interested in being perfect. I suspect perfection doesn't exist but I don't care enough to look closely. I told my self-perfecting friend that, in my flawed view, the greatest risk to her future was not imperfection but extreme boringness.

Perfection doesn't exist. And if it exists then it is for other people. Because perfection is chilly and soulless and naive: a cruel, dull mistress. And the very idea is incredibly emotionally dangerous. What more aggressive method can you think of to set yourself up for failure, to make you feel unloveable *even to yourself*?

Of course, as we grew up we wanted to be extraordinary. We wanted astonishing lives. And then, as it dawned that extraordinary might not be a recipe for happy, well… we wondered. We let go of special and we rejoined the human race. And suddenly, ordinary became a goal in itself. Normal. The irresistible pull of normality. The allure of balance, really. Not 'my shaman will divine my journey' balance. But just the ebb and flow of life until a storm comes – and it surely will – and then a clawing, crawling, gasping battle back to normal.

We travel full circle with regard to normal. As kids, generally, we don't want to be weird but then we begin to look for ways to set ourselves apart slightly. It's not conscious – it's just part of the severing of ties, the throwing off of expectations that adolescence brings. We show off, we act out, we experiment with astonishing and odd and astounding; could be a haircut, a romance, a geographic move, tattoos, politics. We hunt for our tribe, wanting to both belong and to shine, shine, shine. But shimmer, we learn, is brittle, breakable and easily tarnished. And people don't buy it in the end. It reads as hologrammatic. It alienates.

Although we are all uniquely ourselves, we are not *special*. Feeling special is, perhaps, a very efficient way to feel alone. It sets us apart, this specialness. I wonder if a lot of addicts feel special. And a lot of comedians.

Anyway, now that I have grown out of feeling very special, I find that what I am is a highly imperfect person who feels all the time. All the feelings. Not one at a time but ever-shifting, sometimes weightily muddy and other times sharp and stinging, coming and going throughout the day with absolutely no predictability. Exhausting.

But pity the folk who can't bear to feel, who slam the iron doors and reinforce the glass walls. Feelings are a bore. But they are the big connector, the invisible beams that makes us relatable, loving and loveable. Even if we think no one can tell.

Here's what someone said to me the other day when I was floundering and flummoxed and generally panicking about what to do/what to say/how to be. 'You do you,' she said, and it was like a big, fat present tied with a velveteen ribbon of kindness. There is no expectation attached to it and no judgement.

This was someone giving me permission to write my own story, author my own life. Sure, that sounds a bit grandiose and insane, but when we spend so much of our lives playing catch-up and spinning the hamster wheel, 'you do you' hands back control. Because however you choose to 'do you' will be interesting and it will be good enough. It might be frightening. But fear holds no shame. Emphatically not.

We all feel cowardly sometimes. As though, if we were *more* of a person, with *more* backbone, *more* guts, *more* soul, *more* power, we would be living a nobler life. If only we were braver.

Let me tell you something now and forever: just because you are frightened, doesn't mean you aren't brave. You are truly brave. The more fearful you feel, the more heroic you are. Even admitting to feeling scared is brave. We are at our worst when we try to power through, jet-propelled by grim determination and denial. Do that and we run out of road in the end. Do that and we stop blooming and start calcifying. Do that and we deny ourselves the chance of any solace. Cornered. Fear is a perfect indicator that attention must be paid.

Never be ashamed of being frightened. Tell someone you are panicking. They are probably panicking too. We are all fucking panicking. It's one of the reasons that we are wonder women. Not perfect women. Wonder women.

## We're All More Than One Woman

Do you ever feel that you are a complete mystery to yourself? As in: who IS this person? She is unrecognisable from the me of 30 seconds ago. As in: roses are red violets are blue, I'm an enigma to myself and so am I, and so is she, who is also me. Oh God.

This is because we are all more than one woman. Here are just a few of us:

**Dead From The Waist Down Woman**
I may never have sex again. I am perfectly happy and satisfied with the long, grey bush of wisdom. Get that penis away from me...too needy.

**The Pervert**
Everywhere I look I see hot stuff. I may abandon everyone in my life for one night with that hairy guy on the bus. Inexplicable and inappropriate horn descends. A new kind of needy.

**See-Saw Woman**
Not my circus, not my monkeys. Zero fucks left to give. Don't want to hear about the pain. Cut to: I must decant my entire house into bags for the charity shop and I can't bear how beautiful all the children in the world are and that cat is making me cry. And back again.

**Overthinking Woman**
Small problems become total disintegration. Minor rows became destroyed relationships. Tight finances become homelessness. Challenges become vicious enemies. I need to get the hell out of my own way and mutate immediately into...

**Unthinking Woman**
I assume I can't manage lateral thought. But when the situation demands – and the adrenaline soars – I am able to solve problems in nanoseconds. Otherwise known as Get It Done Girl. Except when it comes to tax returns when I become Get Someone Else To Get It Done Girl.

**Fury Female**
I am a bomb about to be detonated. Road rage, bra rage, stop chewing so loudly rage, feeling vulnerable rage, why do I have to do everything rage. RAGE.

**Oh Spiritual One**
I go to one yoga class, brew a warm milk and turmeric then connect with the universe for about 15 seconds. Currently the most inactive part of me.

# It's Only Me

'Hi,' you say. 'Only me!' Oh, but aren't you chirpy? Unintrusive. 'Only me!' Most women I know do it. But not – and this is crucial – any of the alphas: any of the women who have a wholehearted sense of their own value. Not only do women compulsively apologise, but what about compulsively reducing our impact with 'only me-ing' every time we leave a voicemail, ring a doorbell, send an email? It's worse than sorry because it's not an apology, it's a form of self-eradication. 'Only me! Nearly invisible! Just the way you like me!'

What about: 'It's really me!' A call to self-action and self-regard. If it's really me then I'll think just that little bit harder about reacting truthfully and getting what I need from this exchange. These are tiny things but they're kernels of lovely, big, juicy things. 'It's really me' is a very simple, very grounding, comparatively non-wanky affirmation. It's 'I'm loving and loveable and the universe will send me what I need' in digestible form.

These little, bitty phrases steadily reinforce self-limiting beliefs. I mean, it wouldn't feel good to walk into a room and have someone say, 'Oh, it's only her.' If someone said that about your sister or mother or best friend you might take genuine umbrage. What once felt feminine and unobtrusive about 'only me' might have become doormat-ish and unhelpful. After all, it's really you. You are all you've got. And there is beauty in being seen.

# Tiny Ways To Be Outrageous

### 1. Stay Up Past Ten
Remember that world that didn't open for business until after 10pm? (It's still there.) You could dip your toe in it again…let the sleeping beast out of the cage…

### 2. Initiate Sex
Shock all involved parties by vibing Beyoncé and suggesting you get drunk on love in the middle of the day instead of having a conversation about what sort of mortgage renewal you're thinking about. You could try waking him up in the middle of the night (might need to set an alarm) or NOT be angry if he wakes you up. Mind-blowing.

### 3. Add An Extra Hour To The Cleaner
Anyone else feeling slightly aroused at how clean the inside of their fridge would be with this extra time dedicated to the stuff that never gets done?

**4. Have Deliveroo Every Night For A Week**
Everyone gets to order what they want. No more Chinese or Indian debates. All parties appeased. All parties fed like fattened calves. No washing up. No arguments about how to stack the dishwasher. Just a package handed to you as if you were Mariah Carey and had a personal chef.

**5. Take A Valium At 9am And Tell Everyone You Didn't Sleep**
All the accoutrements of no sleep – slurred words, heavy eyes, confusion, yawning – but with lovely feelings of Valium-induced 'It's all going to be fiiiiiine'.

**6. Smoke In Bed Even If You Gave Up In 1997**
Ignore any rising suspicions that this is disgusting and imagine you are Alexis Colby. Did she ever question her choices? No she did not.

**7. Just Have As Much Coffee As You Want – All Day Every Day**
So you'll be totally insane and probably impossible. At least you'll be happy.

**8. Wear A Wig To See Your Therapist**
Turn up to therapy wearing a wig of your choice – something that's in stark contrast to your own hair. Explain that it's really helping you think like a different person.

**9. Use Words Such As Canoodle, Groovy, Humdinger and Monkey Business**
Imagine if you slammed your lady fist on the table in the middle of a meeting and said 'Enough of this monkey business!' Everyone would be dumbstruck.

# Unleash Your Inner Weirdo

All those years of fitting in or cultivating your own brand of oddity. Decades of proving stuff to yourself and to others. The energy wasted wondering if you were loveable, if you were enough. The box ticking: professional, ambitious, presentable.

Well, here's a thought: in a world where 'road-mapping', 'strategy', 'curation' and 'self-perfection' are the wallpaper to our working lives, let your inner weirdo shine through. She is the difference between you and the next guy. In a good way.

Your inner weirdo is the you who doesn't care what you think of you. Your inner weirdo is the FREAK inside you who thinks that it's OK to be you. Who thinks that you'll do. Who finds it amusing when you are a bit of a dick. Who doesn't really do social humiliation. Who has a strange take on things and might nudge you to say it out loud.

Your own personal weirdo is the facet of your character that has freely evolved like a work of art. Not for your weirdo the traumas of childhood or the fear-residue of break-ups. The weirdo is fresh, unfettered. You don't need to look after your weirdo – this isn't 'nurture your inner child' speak. Because your weirdo can look after her damn self. Your weirdo is the part of you that will always be OK so don't worry about her, just unleash her now and again to show the world some True You colours.

# Midult Acronyms

### CHS – Chin Hair Situation

When you casually brush your chin and feel the dagger-like upstart that wasn't there the day before.

### LOLASP – Laughing Out Loud And Slightly Peeing

That pelvic floor is a traitorous bastard. Less taut trampoline, more sagging hammock.

### COL – Crying Out Loud

What's the point of crying if you can't really go for it? Better to get it all out, surely? Trail around the house thumping the furniture, that sort of thing?

### WLTS – Would Like To Sleep

When you haven't slept since before God invented water and have gone into that mental space beyond anger where you are now trying to be humble before the universe in the hope that begging to a higher force for some kind of divine intervention will help.

### OOTD – Outrage Of The Day

WHY did Ocado see fit to replace your Duchy Original biscuits with some Jacob's crackers? WHERE did you put your keys for the millionth time today? HOW is it possible that Tom Hardy is married to someone else?

### FML – Forgot My Life

Friend: How was your Friday night?

You: Went to an all-night party, where I was magnificent from start to finish, knocking back masses of booze, yet still managing to be amusing and devastating, going to bed at dawn, only to have everyone over for breakfast and a debrief.

Also you: (suddenly remembering) Oh, no wait – that's not my life. I was asleep on the sofa at 9.45 with a half-eaten pizza on my lap. The one I finished for breakfast. FML for a moment.

**TBC – To Be Cancelled**
When you agree to drinks you have absolutely no intention of attending.

**ATF – All The Feelings**
Laughing on the outside, crying on the inside. Also feeling angry, but calm. And really, really tired. But happy. And anxious. But optimistic. And brave. Apart from when scared.

**LMAO – Laughing My Anxiety Off**
When you go beyond the fear to a place where it all implodes and you genuinely find the horror funny and then feel slightly better.

# I Need A Swim In Lake Fuck Off

Where is Lake Me? We've Citymapper-ed, we've Googled, we've Waze'd, we've star charted, we've started therapy – and in the process we found Lake Fuck Off. So much for the mellowing that comes with age. So much for being sorted and measured and temperate. So much for moderation and equability. More than ever we find that we care desperately, more than ever we find ourselves swimming in Lake Fuck Off. Come on in…the water's lovely. More than ever we find ourselves fully immersed in Fuck Off Mode.

Fuck Off Mode is basically Activist Mode but the worthiness extracted with a syringe. It is when you say 'enough'. And then you like it. So you keep saying it. And – maybe – you realise that no more Mrs Nice Guy rather suits you. In fact, it's a whole new you. Or, at least, an externalisation of who you truly are. Or who you have become. Fuck Off Mode chimes with Midlulhood. It isn't some kind of foot stamping, know-it-all flounce. It's a seasoned view of injustice, or untruth, or cruelty, combined with a certain surefootedness a million miles from the arrogance of youth. It's empathy blended with power. It's the more we learn, the less we know. It's having the courage to change the things we can. It's knowing that doing something means something. It's no longer standing idly by shaking our heads. Fuck Off Mode has no hysteria, no personal ambition – the button is pressed and cannot be unpressed. It unleashes… belief. There is a sudden clarity; an understating that values matter. Whether you are groped or ignored, disrespected or lied about. Fuck Off Mode takes no prisoners; it doesn't simper. Fuck Off Mode has value. And, if they don't like it, they know what they can do…

## Time For Big Girl Pants

I don't want to pull my socks up, get my act together or give myself a talking to. I don't want to gird my loins, grit my teeth or suck it up. It's all so 'I'm not enough but I'll fake it for as long as I have to'. Sometimes circumstances call for full focus and a drawing together of self. This requires carrot, not stick. This requires inspiration, not degradation. This requires…big girl pants. Metaphorical and magical.

There are times in life when we need to put our big girl pants on. To connect ourselves to the sisterhood through knowing that we have been through some murky stuff and there's probably more in the post but we are one of the grown-ups. We handle things.

Big girl pants are a reminder that we are beautifully qualified, that imposter syndrome will take up no space in our heads – a signpost towards good sense, good humour and clear sightedness. Big girl pants are comfortable because they are truly ours, truly deserved. Hard won. We don't flounce in big girl pants; we don't feel the need to make people sorry; we don't create nutty narratives; we don't tailor reality. This is power.

## Welcome to Midulthood

# MYSTERIES OF THE MIDULT UNIVERSE

1. Why can we no longer remember anything about what we did yesterday but will never forget that shit Max who dumped us for our 'friend' Sarah in 1996? Names haven't been changed.
2. Why do we always wake up at 3am?
3. Why does our salad dressing sometimes not emulsify?
4. Why do we always want to have sex with a new person mid-waxing cycle when NOTHING CAN BE DONE?
5. Why can we never get to the end of an improving current affairs podcast? Even though we have tried really, really hard. And deliberately didn't lie down so we wouldn't fall asleep.
6. Why did we buy that skort thing? Or that cheerful jumper? Or that peasant blouse? Or those shoes that are too small/too high/too ugly for words?
7. Why is the landline ringing?
8. Why did someone leave a voice message?
9. Why can't we bring ourselves to listen to it?
10. Why is no one calling?
11. Why do we think we will be able to resist the 'sharing chips' in the middle of the table?
12. Why did we sleep with so many people? And why are they still alive? And why do they live locally?

## Chapter 14

# ONWARDS AND SIDEWAYS...

I HAVE TROUBLE WITH GOD. Nothing personal, I just don't believe she exists. In fact, in a world where you can't move for meditation and mindfulness, spirituality as a whole presents a problem, largely because the word is so triggering. I do not react well to the self-sloganing 'I'm a very spiritual person'. Is there an element of myth-making about this? An ever-present possibility that they might say, 'Your angry aura is interfering with my chakras'. Plus, they might make you do yoga. Also, do truly spiritual people shout about it over dinner?

What is spirituality anyway? Is it spirituality for spirituality's sake? (I dislike this word so much that I'm typing it again and again as a kind of reverse aversion therapy, which is not working.) Is it about belief? Or, is it, really and truly, about hope? About the power of possibility. That is one hell of a higher power.

But do we dare to hope? It's a big ask. Particularly when our tone around hope is so laced with cynicism. 'I hope you know what you're doing,' says the friend who thinks you are asking for trouble. 'I hope you find a parking space,' says another who thinks you are mad to drive. We articulate a kind of insurance policy against disappointment with a sighing, 'I see that this is a triumph of hope over experience.'

We try, as grown-ups (!), to get to grips with the difference between hope and fantasy. The latter has a valuable place in our lives because we can really go to town and weave that dreamy narrative about spending the lottery money or moving to a tropical island. Fantasy is without expectation; we can live alongside a fantasy, knowing it is fiction, tweaking it as we go – like a Pinterest board. But hope is about things we truly desire that might be attainable: the baby, the job, the clean bill of health, the knowledge that we are loved. And so hope feels perilous. Which is why I have reframed it as possibility; the possibility that everything might be alright in the end. Thinking hope rather than feeling hope. Living in a hope-ful space rather than a dread-ful one. Trying to train my mind in such a way that it starts to take…just making hope available to myself. Just imagining the possibility that the universe might send good things my way.

A connection to possibility can translate as freedom. Freedom to sit back and open your eyes rather than pant and squint. To wonder about the future rather than resent its mystery. Panic does not protect us. If we worry, the outcome will certainly not be better and very likely be worse. Anxiety shrinks our world, backs us into a corner, closes off options and opportunities.

Of course, there is meditation and there's medication and there's therapy and friendship. There's conversation and there's communication and there's alcohol. But sometimes it's tough to try to choose. When we're at a loss. No morale in the bank. No perspective to call on.

Here's a humble suggestion from one who's been around the block: find yourself a piece of sky. Doesn't have to be blue or sunny, just has to be sky. Because sky represents the power of possibility. It is a – quite literally – higher power delivered without the need to work on a spiritual life if that feels too demanding. The sky is bigger than us and it is not a stretch to look to it for solace because it is RIGHT THERE. And who knows what is coming? Sun, rain, lightning, clouds. Good or bad, they move and pass on. And, much like the sea, it never fails to stir us. Darkness, dusk, dawn – the sky pulls us into the present.

Sky is space. It allows room for bruises to fade and hearts to howl or to leap and sing with joy. The best thing I can do when it's all very nearly too, too much, is to go out into my postage-stamp-sized garden, lie flat on my back, keep my eyes open and wonder at my own little piece of sky.

## Don't Panic, It's Only The Apocalypse

My boyfriend is 20 minutes late; he cycles, so obviously he is dead, mowed down by a lorry at that horrible roundabout. But there is no time for sadness, I have already gone into Apocalypse Mode. I am thinking, did we sort out the life insurance, what about the mortgage? It will be a bit lonely, but at least there is always the Ocado man to talk to on a Sunday evening.

My train is stuck outside the station; well, obviously someone has blown it up. Radio 3 goes crackly and then silent; everyone in the world has been felled by some terrible virus, everyone except me, and in no time I will be like WALL-E, roaming the Earth, tidying up, with nothing but a wind-up VHS and my old video of *Excalibur*. I am hardwired for catastrophe, I always have been, and for a long time assumed everyone else was too, until I met my boyfriend and realised that there were really people out there who think that the world is a benign place and the worst thing isn't necessarily going to happen.

Freaks.

Yes, some of the places my brain takes me might seem illogical, but it is a powerful form of self-protection, because when he walks through the door, when the train steams into a weirdly intact station, when the radio starts up again with a lovely bit of Vaughan Williams, I am happier than any of you. And the apocalypse *will* come one day, I know it, I am waiting for it. To be honest I would be a bit annoyed if it didn't.

# Whatever Gets You Through The Week

Sometimes only woo woo will do. When we've exhausted Western medicine and therapeutic protocol and every day is a long, dark night of the soul, frankly, we'll try anything.

### Positive Visualisation

See yourself in the house, that job, having sex with that man. Really see it, imagine it, fill in the details. Believe it is happening. Send that potentiality out into the world. The seed has been sown. You are making it happen. Apparently.

### Crystals

We have bought 'crystals' for a vast amount of money, even though we were so broke it was pitta bread for lunch. We have blown our many cares into them, like they might be able to disperse our woes to the winds. We have one by the bed for more mysterious dreams, we keep them in our bra when we go out for 'protection'. We believe in this shit even though there is no evidence for it at all. Because we want to. Because it helps.

### Horoscopes

Some read a horoscope every day. Those in the know wait for Astrology Zone to drop at the start of the month (ooh, it's the 28th...soon, soon!). We speed-read it first and then read more slowly, savouring the future, hunting for the relevant stuff. We get annoyed when the things promised don't happen and feel smug when they sort of, kind of, vaguely do.

### Talk To The Moon

'Please help, everything is a bit shit right now, my boss is a cunt, I've had the same spot for a month, I am in so much debt I am actually scared to look at my bank balance, I feel lonely, I don't know what to do, and you look so bright and wise and powerful...' Listen, humans have been doing this for about ten thousand years, don't knock it.

### Reiki

We sat in a dark basement room and closed our eyes while a 'healer' with an unidentifiable accent hovered her hands over our body. Sometimes we felt nothing, sometimes we felt hot spots, like there was a ray of heat being blasted through our body and it made us momentarily awed and breathless. Sometimes we saw intense colours and fractal-like shapes. What was going on, we asked afterwards. 'The energy of the universe flows through my hands into your body, helping to heal you and unblock you,' she said. So that was £90 well spent.

### Frog Poison

We had been feeling a bit 40 per cent for months, no energy, no vim. Detoxification might help, someone said. 'I did this frog poison thing and I felt so amazing,' someone else said, and she had really clear skin and bright eyes…So we went to Lewes and spent £200 to sit in a garden shed while someone pricked our shoulder a few times (ouch) and applied the poison. We have never seen so much vomit…But a week later, we did feel sort of better, sort of purged. Next stop, ayahuasca in Peru.

### Shaman

She comes from Hampshire but she lived for three years in a tiny village in the Andean rainforest being trained by an ancient Inca wiseman. She waved branches over our tummy, billowed smoke around our head, sprinkled rose water onto our hair and told us to imagine that we were riding a unicorn. We did. We were! We were riding a unicorn!! We were flying over snowy mountain ranges on a unicorn!! Then we had to get the bus home.

### Tarot

We bought a deck because we liked the pictures. We read the book, because why not? And now, when we are feeling a bit scared or weird or confused, we get them out and give ourselves a reading. And it makes us feel a bit more in control. Ah ha, there is the Sun, everything is going to be amazing and our endeavours will be successful. Ah ha, there is Justice, those nasty people who have thwarted us WILL get their comeuppance. Ah, there are the Lovers…And the minute our friends found out they wanted a reading too.

### Church

Because singing in a beautiful room on a Sunday morning is kind of fun. And sitting quietly listening to a man in a dress talking about good and bad is kind of interesting. And it is helpful to be reminded of all the times we have sat in churches – births, weddings and deaths. Beginnings, middles and endings.

## Sayings We Pray Are True

Clichés – when they don't irritate us – tend to make us feel better. Comforting in their familiarity. We rely on them like…zebra crossings, in that everyone knows what they mean and there is a larger act of trust involved. But what if it's all lies? Please let the following be true…

1.  It is what it is. Well what if it isn't? What if it is something else entirely? Say a wolf in sheep's clothing? Or a Greek bearing a gift? Perhaps it would be better to say 'It could be what it might be.' And then shrug.
2.  The universe will provide. What if it doesn't? What if the universe leaves you out in the gutter of life like a single shoe?
3.  You only get given what you can handle. Thanks a lot, guys. I was kind of at capacity one migraine, one leaking roof and two bad boyfriends ago.
4.  Plenty more fish in the sea. What if someone got the last decent cod? And now they're all gone. No more cod. Oh Cod.
5.  Lightning doesn't strike twice. I think this has already been disproved.
6.  Karma will get him in the end. This had just better be true.
7.  You only live once. Thanks Buddha but please NOT again.
8.  This too will pass. Hopefully. But it's also possible that we are probably always going to feel like this. Only slightly different day-to-day, hour-to-hour. Nuanced rather than transformed.
9.  What doesn't kill you makes you stronger. Wait a second, how much stronger do we need to be?
10. It will be OK in the end. The end.

# Mantras For Midults

### Am I Being Childish? Good!

Yes, this might be a tantrum; yes, this could be classed as undignified; yes, you may have flicked that book off the table on purpose; yes, you may be saying 'But what about ME?'; and yes, you are probably a little bit vengeful and definitely not considered or considerate but sometimes you just have to be. *blows raspberry*

### If It's Not Going Right, Go Left

So you took the road less travelled and now you don't know where the fuck you are. Need we remind you that the definition of insanity is doing the same thing over and over again, flogging a dead horse and all that. But don't stop completely. Get back on the horse (a live one though) and change direction. Sounds so easy, doesn't it?

### My Alone Time Is For Your Safety...

If you find that your people are funny about the idea that you want to be alone more than you want to hang out with them, then perhaps it might help if you show them the mental doodles you are doing of pushing them off a cliff. Or maybe not. Just lock the door.

## I'm Going In

You are an astronaut and a bit of your rocket is on fire. You need to save your inner child and this metaphor is a bit annoying, isn't it? Anyway you are going in. You've strapped on your oxygen mask, one of the minor Baldwin brothers is by your side and you are first through the vacuum-locked door. You are brave and can handle your booze and your tax return. *spits*

## It's Not Me. It's You

Sometimes it is them. It just is. Them. Arseholes. You are fine-ish. You meditate and you see a therapist and you try really hard. And they are still complete dicks.

## Today I Face My Demons...Poor Them

For the days when you are so strong, so powerful, so flowing with lady juju that all those naysayers, all the sneaky little voices in your head, all the folks that said you couldn't do it, well they are TOAST. Mmmm...hungry now.

## You Weren't Built In A Day

They say that all the cells in our bodies renew themselves every seven years. So seven years ago you were an entirely different person. Fourteen years ago another person before that. You are like one of those scary algorithms that mutates as it gains knowledge. You don't have to know everything. You don't have to know anything. OK, some things. But mostly, just give yourself a break. You're still mutating...

## Life Is Tough. So Are You

This is for the days when you are sick of shit being thrown at you and just making you stronger. When you realise that you have a ton of unhealthy coping mechanisms to unravel but hell, on the plus side they are coping mechanisms. You are coping. And now in caps: YOU ARE COPING. Hell, you've had waxes tougher than this, bitch.

## Shift Happens

You might not believe this right now but with a little bit of work and a little bit of space and a little bit of time and some awfully painful bits, there are occasional tectonic plate movements inside that open up new neural pathways. And you see a hurt differently, or a past injustice, and you feel minutely changed all of sudden. A sort of tiny Heimlich manoeuvre in the heart. Nice.

## Bury Them With A Smile

So today is difficult, difficult, lemon difficult. But you are not sour, you are sweet.

You are carving out ways of relating to the world. You are smiling. And they weren't expecting that. Fuckers.

## What Could Possibly Go Wrong?
We know what you are thinking: 'What complete maniac would ask this question?' 'What insane fate-tempter would send out such a challenge?' Slightly regretting it now.

## Perfection? You Can Keep It
You are under no obligation to be the same person you were yesterday or even five minutes ago. You are under no obligation to wear matching knickers and bras and always excel at your job, exercise regularly and text everyone back. Perfection is for other people.

## Why Wouldn't You?
Why wouldn't you order a pizza instead of cooking? Why wouldn't you say you can't go out because you are really tired? Why wouldn't you start your own business? Why wouldn't you buy the red bikini or book a holiday with your best friend or have five coffees in a row? How much coffee is too much coffee? Sorry, I don't understand the question.

## Never Ever Give Up On Your Hair
Roots, that crunchy dryness, the terrible parched orange from years of dyeing, sorry colouring, sorry enhancing. So what if the time between hair appointments is getting smaller and smaller? So what if you wake up every morning like you've been wrestling with an alligator and you suspect your hairdresser wants to give you a 'practical' haircut? Never ever give up on your hair.

## I Am Listening
OK universe. I am here, I am present (sort of), I am in the moment (is this the moment, I think I am in the moment, am I in the moment? Or is the moment over there?) and I am listening. Listening for the signs, ready for the riches, looking for the guidance, I am ready and listening. Still listening. Hello?

## Idiots Happen
You can't hate everyone annoying because you end up toxifying your soul. You don't have to love them either. Dickheads off a duck's back, basically. Energy is finite; don't waste yours...

**I Am Dynamic, I Am Invincible, I Am Exhausted**
For those days when you have done all the paperwork, made the bed, sewn on a button, given a talk, delivered a report, had six fights (three of them by yourself, in the shower) and now you are just going to order a Chinese and eat it in the bath.

**Don't Set Yourself On Fire To Keep Someone Else Warm**
Of course I can be funny, brilliant, kind, sexy, tend to your every need…oh no hold on, I am combusting. And I seem to be the only one bringing anything to the party. Go away.

**Onwards And Sideways**
Static is no good. Rut is bad. But sometimes we go wonky before we soar. Momentum is the thing; measured momentum. Understanding that life is made up of many chapters and that this will not be the one to derail you. That is not an option. Gently does it.

## Welcome to Midulthood

# A MIDULT WISHLIST

### 1. A Bag Of Healthy Coping Mechanisms
To feel a little less trapped in an emotional pinball machine.

### 2. Comfortable Shoes That Don't Look Comfortable
So we don't look/feel/behave like Nurse Ratched. So we don't squeak down life's corridors looking like we might lobotomise anyone who annoys us. Although…

### 3. Higher Tolerance For Caffeine
It would be nice not to feel that strange back of the eyeball tightening after just three triple-shot-soya lattes. We just want all of the awake with none of the heart attack please.

### 4. A New List
We are declaring a list amnesty. A clean slate. No recriminations. No regrets. Throw the old lists away. They are no longer working documents. Start again. Dare to hope.

### 5. To Be Better At Saying No
Or even just, 'I am terribly sorry I don't think I will be able to do that because *inserts brilliant excuse that doesn't sound like an excuse*.'

### 6. Some Spontaneity
Yes, routine is comforting. Yes, we like our sofa best. But what about some fly-by-the-seat-of-our-pants woohoo? Just once or twice a year. With planning. Sorry.

### 7. Cash Flow
A little breathing space would be fine. Not diamonds or private planes. But maybe a side return and some new boots. Plus new knickers. Also winter sun. And taxis.

### 8. To Have Not Slept With The IT Guy
Please can you just wipe that off our naughty list? It was 15 years ago and our self-esteem was not throbbing with good health at the time. So, if we agree that it didn't happen, then it didn't happen, right? Can we agree on that?

### 9. A Better Memory
Because it's getting a bit embarrassing to start a really impressive sentence, replete with many subordinate clauses and a rather unique point of view, and then…sorry, what was I saying?

### 10. Happy Endings
With proper jewellery.

# The End

We have no way of knowing how you feel after what we've just put you through. Maybe it's been an ordeal. Perhaps it's been a hoot. Most likely it's been a mixture. But we'd like to leave you with this thought, you magnificent Midults: none of us have come this far to only come this far. Of course it's not the end.

# It Takes A Village – Meet Team Midult

### Gavanndra Hodge

Gav is an editor of such distinction that we can but kneel at the altar of her brilliance. No one else in the world is called this (her father made up the name while high in the Seventies) and no one else in the world is like her. So that's OK then. She has been the custodian of this book and of our sanity (and, let's face it, who wants *that* job?). A minxy bluestocking, Gav has read more books than all of you put together, is a witchy, wild-child, Latin-loving classical scholar and science fiction fiend. Her dazzling first novel will be out imminently. Be afraid.

### Clare Bennett

When it comes to writing, Clare is the silent partner in The Midult. Laughably talented and ridiculously egoless, she is responsible for the 'Conversations with', the 'Adventures in Insomnia' and the 'I'm more X than you' series, not to mention myriad other brilliances. Amazing considering she hasn't slept since 1998. Devoted to violent blondeness and leopard print, she has a laugh that has actually shattered glass (we've seen it happen. It's awesome). She is a peerless writer and a peerless person. She talks too much about both *The Odyssey* and The Kardashians and hand-makes all her Christmas presents, which may or may not be because of her massive crush on Jesus. We wish her luck with that.

### Jinny Yeon

Her name is not even Jinny. Her name is an unpronounceable secret. It is not an understatement to say that she is the backbone of the entire operation, running our lives, brains and words with a ruthless brilliance. She is the puppeteer. The organ grinder. The Sauron to our Orc army. The BBC is the only channel she watches and she cannot deal with any kind of weather. She has a vast heart, a short temper, a monumental intellect, an assassin's inscrutability and an unfortunate *tendresse* for belVita Breakfast Bars. If she ever left us, we would disappear and it would be like we'd never existed.

**Sara McCorquodale**

Corky is tiny and Scottish. Freckly too. There are few things in life more charming than the way she says 'tiara'. What this woman can do with plaits goes far beyond human understanding. Her wholehearted and incredibly imaginative handling of The Midult's social media has been a wonder to behold. Chirrupy, sunny and wry ('I love it like Whitney loved crack,' she once said with an adorable smile), she is a workaholic entrepreneur. Her influencer tech tool CORQ promises to be dangerously successful. From (just outside) Glasgow to infinity and beyond...via Chiswick.

**Alexandra Borthwick**

Alexandra is the power behind the exhaustive and tear-jerkingly useful Midult directories on curtain makers, jewellery menders, plumbers, handymen and clothes fixers to name but a few. She will not reveal her sources. She unhelpfully fucked off to Scotland last year – hence the '24 Things You Only Know Once You've Moved To The Country' list. She has a fantasy about checking into the Premier Inn in Hammersmith and spending the night on her own. Wild. She hates parking and it makes her homicidal, so it's probably a good thing that she now lives in a bothy/castle. We don't know which. Because we have yet to be invited.

# Acknowledgements

Annabel and Emilie have spent years fantasising about writing the acknowledgements in a book that they have actually written in real life. Now that day has dawned, they are completely paralysed, so if they have forgotten anyone they are really sorry. They are always slightly sorry.

Really it's our agent Zoe King who is to blame for all this – she is the one who forced us to write the book. So if you hated it, we can give you her phone number.

The sensational Alison Starling at Octopus – thank you for wanting this book, for all the brownies you let Emilie eat and all the times you let Annabel shout. And all the fabulous team at Octopus: Denise Bates, Caroline Brown (one of our earliest adopters), Sybella Stephens and Charlotte Cole (for such humane copy-editing), the inscrutable Jonathan Christie (who only looks a little bit like Richard Hammond), Allison Gonsalves in Production and UK Sales Director Kevin Hawkins (we love you Kevin). We couldn't have asked for a better home.

Huge gratitude to the artist Eliza Hopewell – who beautifully captured the madness on the book's decorated endpapers – because she is a bit mad too. And properly brilliant.

As the saying goes, it takes a village. Deep breath: the incomparable Clive Rumens who believed in us from the beginning. Sasha Slater at the *Saturday Telegraph Magazine* (who generously gave us our column), Laura Powell (who has to deal with our annoyingness). Laura Weir at *ES Magazine* (for being our champion), and Charlotte Ross and Jackie Annesley for being our cheerleaders. Not to mention the marvellous Aaron Bennett who built themidult.com with his bare hands.

Special thanks to Joanna Plant, Emma Loach, Kate Roskill and Dr Kate Carpenter for reading this when it was all over the place and for convincing us to keep going. To Liz Wildi for breaking things down so beautifully. And all the marvellous Midults who came to our dinners and opened their hearts.

Annabel would particularly like to thank Bluey for being Bluey, Tom for Pink Wine Baby Night and all that followed, and Alexander because we survived. And of course, Daisy, Jemima, Lucy and Porks for never letting go.

Emilie would also like to thank Isabel (always), James, her rebel girls Esme and Agnes, Billy and Chris Hodge who makes everything possible.

And huge and heartfelt thanks to the mothers... Pamela Rivkin and Patsie McMeekan. And not just because we have to.